Brickyards
to
Graveyards

SUNY series in the Anthropology of Work

June C. Nash, editor

Brickyards to Graveyards

From Production to Genocide in Rwanda

Villia Jefremovas

State University of New York Press

Published by
State University of New York Press, Albany

© 2002 State University of New York

All rights reserved

Printed in the United States of America

No part of this book may be used or reproduced in any manner whatsoever without written permission. No part of this book may be stored in a retrieval system or transmitted in any form or by any means including electronic, electrostatic, magnetic tape, mechanical, photocopying, recording, or otherwise without the prior permission in writing of the publisher.

For information, address State University of New York Press,
90 State Street, Suite 700, Albany, NY 12207

Production by Michael Haggett
Marketing by Michael Campochiaro

Library of Congress Cataloging-in-Publication Data

Jefremovas, Villia.
  Brickyards to graveyards : from production to genocide in Rwanda / Villia Jefremovas.
    p. cm. — (SUNY series in anthropology of work)
  Includes bibliographical references and index.
  ISBN 0-7914-5487-8 (alk. paper) — ISBN 0-7914-5488-6 (pbk. : alk. paper)
  1. Labor—Rwanda. 2. Working class—Rwanda. 3. Rwanda—Economic conditions. 4. Rwanda—Social conditions. 5. Genocide—Rwanda. I. Title. II. Series.

HD8795 .J44 2002
338.4'766673'0967571—dc21

                                                                        2002070716

10 9 8 7 6 5 4 3 2 1

For Joachim and Larysa

Contents

Acknowledgments		ix
List of Illustrations and Tables		xi
1	Introduction—Rwanda and the Field Sites	1
2	Making Bricks and Roof Tiles in Rwanda: Technology and Process	21
3	Making Bricks and Roof Tiles in Rwanda: Labor Organization	35
4	Land Tenure, Common Property, and Labor and Power: Precolonial, Colonial, and Postcolonial Transformations	59
5	"Your Patron Begets You": Household Reproduction, Gender and Domestic Relations, and Access to Family Labor	79
6	Loose Women, Virtuous Wives, and Timid Virgins: Class, Gender, and the Control of Resources	97
7	Brickyards Turn to Graveyards	109
Appendix A. Various Chronologies for the Rwandan Kings		127
Appendix B. European Contact and the German Colonial Period		129
Appendix C. The Belgian Colonial Period		131
Appendix D. Prestations, *Corvées*, Taxes, and Obligations (1898–1940)		133

Notes	135
Bibliography	145
Index	155

Acknowledgments

My greatest debt is to the Rwandan peasants and entrepreneurs who so patiently answered my questions, and to Béatrice Ntabomvura, my research assistant, whose diligence, interest in this research, capacity to criticize and to question, and ability to follow up new insights contributed in immeasurable ways to the quality of the material we collected. My profound thanks go to my husband, Joachim Voss, who provided the photographs that have been included in this book, read endless drafts, argued over interpretations, and supported me, literally and figuratively, while I wrote this book. Thanks also go to my daughter, Larysa Voss, who lived with this research project, in its various incarnations, and whose pride in my work has always inspired me. I am very grateful to the Ontario Graduate Scholarship program that funded my research in 1984 and to the International Development Research Centre "Young Canadian Researcher Award" that funded my research from 1984 to 1985.

Christie Brown, Innocent Butare, Marie-Bernard Kiyuku Butare, James Fairhead, Bernadette Guyon-Benoit, Angelique Haugerud, Betsy Lamb, Winnie Lem, Fiona Mackenzie, Johan Pottier, Joanne Prindiville, Bob Shenton, and Gavin Smith provided endless discussion and insights. Glen Bornais, Marlon Drayton, and Joanne Prindiville helped me in my hour of need. Melchior and Marie Kanyamebwa, with their capacity to look beyond the rhetoric of the government-sponsored history of the day and their ardent interest in the precolonial state, opened my eyes to the ideological pitfalls that await any scholar of Rwanda and made me aware of the complexity of Rwandan history and politics. Monique Mukamusoni and Devota Mukashyaka kept my life in order, and were second mothers to my daughter. I have missed their lively good spirits every day since I left Rwanda. During the genocide I turned to Catherine and David Newbury to pool information and knowledge, and to share the anguish of those days. Their generosity in sharing their work, their insights, and their passion for Rwanda have sustained me. Nevertheless, the opinions expressed in this book and any mistakes and inaccuracies are my sole responsibility.

List of Illustrations and Tables

MAPS

1. Rwanda. Political Map (1983) — 5
2. Location of Field Sites in Southern Rwanda — 8
3. Location of Field Sites in Northwest Rwanda — 14
4. Rwanda. Principal Ethnic/Political Massacres or Attacks (1991–1993) — 116

SCHEMATA

1. Schema of Gatovu Brickyards and Common Property Land Use — 9
2. Schema of Ngoma Brickyards and Common Property Land Use — 11
3. Schema of Huye and Common Property Land Use — 13
4. Schema of Pfunda and Common Property Land Use — 15
5. Schema of Gisa and Common Property Land Use — 17

FIGURES

1. Loading a Clamp Brick Kiln — 23
2. Trimming a Semidry Tile — 28

TABLES

1. Comparative Costs of Brick and Roof Tile Production — 32
2. Informants Selling Food Crops in the South and the North — 91

1

Introduction—
Rwanda and the Field Sites

In 1984, when this study of brick and roof tile industries began, Rwanda, with its leader, Juvenal Habyarimana, was the darling of the world community, the development agencies, and the media. A peaceful African backwater, it appeared to have a government that was relatively uncorrupt, a people who were hardworking, and an economy that was booming. Because of my interest in labor organization and small industries, I decided to conduct my research on the small brick and roof tile industries found in virtually every marsh in the country. These industries, which used European technologies that had been adapted to the local conditions, had found a growing market in the building boom fueled by the new economic prosperity. An article in the *Toronto Star* epitomized the world's opinion of Rwanda and its government. It began, "Diplomats based in this tiny mist-shrouded, mountainy country call it a 'model of development for all of Africa.'" It went on to laud its peoples' "proud and sophisticated demeanor"; its annual economic growth of "5 per cent"; its president, a "military man . . . [who ruled in] the tradition of a benign king" albeit in a "limited democracy"; and praised it for avoiding the "ritual tribal bloodbaths" of its neighbor, Uganda. It was a country in which "even shabby dress [did] not seem to be tolerated" (*Toronto Star*, October 6, 1984). A decade later Rwanda was the byword for genocide and evil. The overidealized picture drawn by diplomats, development experts, and the press had shattered completely. The brickyards in this study had turned into graveyards and most of the specific brick and roof tile industries in this study no longer existed.

This book grew out of the realization that the political, economic, cultural, and social factors that created the conditions under which brick and production took place were also factors that provided some of the preconditions for the genocide. This study of these industries provides a lens through which the lead-up to the events that so horrified the world in 1994 can be viewed.

The conditions and the history, which shaped the labor organization in these small industries, coupled with civil war and structural adjustment, also molded the politics of genocide in Rwanda. Labor organization in Rwanda was, and continues to be, embedded in political, economic, and social relations created by local history and local politics. These conditions have not changed significantly since the Rwandan Patriotic Front took power in 1994. These industries provide a means to examine the transformation of gender,[1] class, and power relations during the precolonial, colonial, and postcolonial periods, and to consider the explosive effects of these transformations on Rwandan culture and society. The precolonial conquest and centralization of power, the overlay of racism and exclusion created by the European colonialism, and the development of the postcolonial regimes produced the class, power, gender, and regional relations that were critical to the form taken by the genocide, are also central to understanding the nature of these industries and forms of labor organization.

The precolonial and colonial history of Rwanda is not about the destruction of previously egalitarian traditional structures by European imperialism or by the penetration of a capitalist economy. Rather, it is about the growth of hierarchical institutions within a fundamentally nonegalitarian system characterized by unequal social relations and strong regional distinctions. It is a history of conquest and assimilation, of the incorporation of different regions into the precolonial kingdom of Rwanda under varying circumstances, of the creation of ethnic groups based on the organization of economic life, and of the transformation of a largely ceremonial kingship into a centralized politically and economically powerful absolute monarchy. European colonialism recast the complex political and economic relations that were beginning to be phrased in terms of ethnicity in the late precolonial period into a simplified caste system based on "racial" categories that determined access to power, education, and status, as well as access to land and labor. The Social Revolution[2] of 1959–1962 led to the codification of "tradition" by the Hutu elite, who took power and entrenched a very different system of land tenure between the different regions of Rwanda. This revolution lodged power into the hands of the Hutu elite from the south. This in turn fueled the overthrow of the First Republic by a faction of the army drawn from the Hutu elite of the north. Since the reign of King Rwabugiri (1860–1895), power in Rwanda has been based on regional and ethnic exclusion.

Ethnicity and power have been intertwined throughout Rwandan history. Precolonial Rwanda was a kingdom in which there were three ethnic groups, the Tutsi, the Hutu, and the Twa. At the time of European contact, a few Tutsi aristocratic clans dominated the elite. While there were some Hutu lords, the majority of the Hutu population were peasants. The Twa, who comprised less than 1 percent of the population, were predominantly hunter-gatherers or potters, although a few found their way into the courts. However, these distinctions can be misleading as these three groups were not, and are not distinguished by, language, culture, religion, or geography.[3] Although Rwanda has been characterized as a "caste system" in much of the colonial literature, this characterization is inaccurate. The majority of Tutsi were commoners, members of commoner clans, and like the majority of Hutu, they were peasants.[4] They spoke the same language, Kinyarwanda, they lived interspersed throughout the country,[5] and they practiced the same religion. Because of the history of conquest in Rwanda, the members of the three groups within a region often share more common cultural traits with each other than they do with members of the same "ethnic group" from other regions. Moreover, all the patrilineal clans of Rwanda were made up of Tutsi, Hutu, and Twa lineages. Although Rwanda began as a German colony in 1899, from 1916 until independence in 1961 a Belgian Protectorate governed through a tiny Tutsi elite. After the revolution of 1959–1962, a Hutu elite held power through two regimes but they represented different regions of Rwanda. The First Republic (1961–1973) was dominated by a central and southern Hutu elite, while the Second Republic (1973–1994) was dominated by a northern Hutu elite. Since 1994 the Tutsi-dominated Rwandan Patriotic Front, most of whom come from the 1959 diaspora, have held power and local Hutu and Tutsi have been virtually excluded from access to power.

Three conundrums have characterized Rwandan political history and governance: the centralization of power into the hands of a tiny minority, the intolerance of opposition, and the problem of succession. These conundrums have established the dynamics of inequality; have set the conditions of access to land, labor, and power; and have fashioned a society in which access to power and resources was, and continues to be, based on ethnic and regional politics and clientage. These factors also underpin the most striking features of the Rwandan enterprises that I studied: the relationship between clientalism[6] and access to the means of production, the widespread practice of piecework, the lack of family labor in both big and small industries, and the role of women's labor in agriculture in reproducing labor for industry. As this book will show, these dynamics also made a genocide possible. Let us begin by placing this study of Rwanda into its geographic, demographic, and economic context.

RWANDA

Rwanda is a small, landlocked country covering 26,340 km² in highland central Africa situated mostly between 1,000 m and 4,500 m above sea level and bordering Lake Kivu. It borders on Burundi in the south, Uganda in the north, the Democratic Republic of Congo (then Zaïre) in the west, and Tanzania in the east (see map 1). The terrain of Rwanda varies quite dramatically. The northwestern region is mountainous, the central region is a hilly plateau, the northwest is a rolling savanna land, while the southeast is predominantly low-lying marshland. There is a great range in altitude, from 1,000 m to 4,500 m (Battistini and Prioul 1981:9–31). Most regions of Rwanda have marshy areas that yield clay and most contain small brick and tile enterprises. In 1983 when this research was begun, Rwanda was divided into ten *prefectures*.[7]

Rwanda is one of the most densely populated countries in Africa. The population[8] was estimated by the Rwandan government to be 6.7 million in 1988 (MINIPLAN 1988) and at around 7,200,000 in 1999 (World Guide 2001:461). Over 90% of the population is rural. In 1978, 41% of the population lived in areas with a population density of more than 300 km^2, 47% lived in areas with a population density between 150 km and 300 km^2, and 12% lived in areas with a population density less than 150 km^2 (Prioul 1981:61–80). In 1979 United Nations Educational, Scientific and Cultural Organization (UNESCO) figures posited an average population density of 336 km^2 with areas as high as 457 km^2 (D. Newbury 1999:32). As David Newbury points out, these "average figures veiled significant differences" between *prefectures* and in land holdings (D. Newbury 1999:32). In 1984, the National Agricultural Survey estimated that "15% of the farmers owned half of the land, especially in the provinces *[prefectures]* of rural Kigali, Gitarama, and Gikongoro" (Uvin 1998:113). Newbury argues that in 1993 "in some areas of Gisenyi *[prefecture]*, 70% of homesteads held less than one-half hectare and a full 45% had less than one-quarter hectare" (D. Newbury 1999:32). From the 1980s on, there was a growing pattern of land concentration into the hands of the politically powerful and a growth of landlessness (Uvin 1998:112–113).

At the time of this study (1984–1988), coffee, tea, pyrethrum (the basis for a natural pesticide), and cinchona (the basis for quinine), as well as development aid, were the main sources of external revenue, and subsistence agriculture was the most important economic activity of the majority of the population. Cash crops occupied 4% of the country's cultivated land, but provided 92% of the export revenues. Food crops, primarily for household consumption, were grown on the remaining cultivated land. The main food crops were bananas, beans, manioc (cassava), sorghum, sweet potatoes, and potatoes. Five percent of these crops were grown for sale (Jones and Egli 1984:12–14; EIU 1991:47). Development aid became an increasingly important source of foreign revenues from the mid-1970s on, growing from 60% in 1977 to over 90% in 1993. Foreign debt grew from 16% of the Gross National Product (GNP) in 1980 to 32% of the GNP in 1990 (Uvin 1998:41, 54).

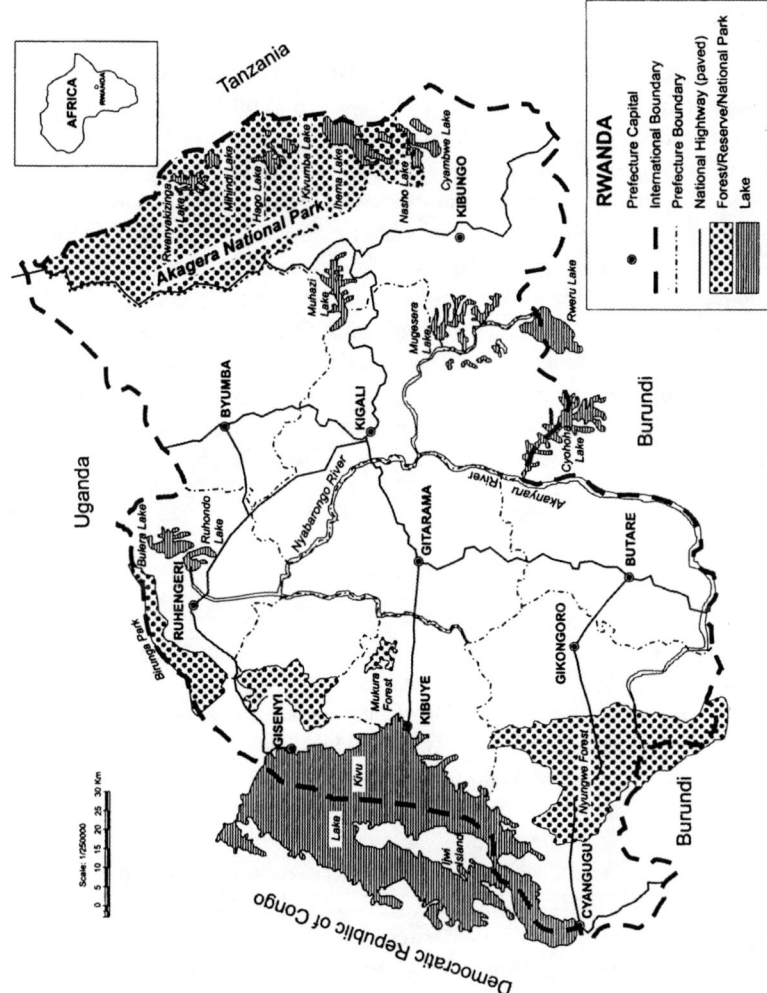

MAP 1. Rwanda. Political Map (1983)

Formal sector industry and manufacturing were very limited. The 1991 Economist Intelligence Unit (EIU) reports that the industrial and services sectors "accounted for only 5% of employment in 1960" and had increased to 9% by 1981. Three percent of the labor force worked in industry, 4% in services, and 93% in agriculture (EIU 1991:44–46). The Gross Domestic Product (GDP) in 1987 was comprised of agriculture (37%), manufacturing (16%), other industry (7%), and services (40%). Of the 16% of the GDP generated by manufacturing, food processing (tea, coffee, beer, soft drinks, sugar, and oil) accounted for 10% and other manufacturing (cigarettes, matches, soap, plastic shoes, agricultural implements, and textiles) the remaining 6%. These figures do not include any informal sector activities, primarily tailoring, brick and roof tile making, adobe brick production, and pottery. It is impossible to estimate the number of enterprises involved in these forms of manufacturing. A 1989 proposal by the Université National de Rwanda to the International Development Research Centre (IDRC) estimated that there are 5,000 artisanal brick industries in Rwanda, manufacturing approximately 60,000,000 bricks a year (IDRC 1989:8). This estimate illustrates the problem of statistics in Rwanda; roof tile industries, far more extensive than brick industries, were not included in these figures, although virtually every peasant home in Rwanda has a tiled roof.

FIELD SITES

The research was conducted in two of the most populated regions of Rwanda: Gisenyi *prefecture* in the northwest, and Butare *prefecture* in the south.[9] The most intensive fieldwork was done in the *secteur* of Gatovu in the *commune* of Ruhashya in Butare *prefecture*,[10] but comparative work was done in two urban locations in the city of Butare and in two rural locations in Gisenyi *prefecture*. The research in the comparative sites focused exclusively on brick and tile makers,[11] while the research in the main field site also investigated households not engaged in brick and tile making.

The locations were chosen because of the great differences in land tenure, in political clout, and in the scale of the brick and tile industries between the northwest and the south. The field sites within each region were chosen because of the different markets they served and the different patterns of land-use they represented.

Field Sites in Butare *Prefecture*

There were three field sites in Butare *prefecture* (see map 2). The first, the *secteur* of Gatovu, was located in a rural area and catered to a rural market. The second was in the *commune urbaine* of Huye and catered to an affluent urban market. The third was located in the *commune urbaine* of Ngoma and catered to a poor peasant market. All of these enterprises operated only in the dry seasons that fell between the two rainy seasons during which the entrepreneurs and laborers worked on their farms. All used public lands for digging the clay and were confined to digging in small pits that were interspersed with small agricultural plots (see schemata 1–5). There was considerable variation in both the scale of enterprises, the products produced, and the strategies employed by the owners and workers in the different marshes and valley bottoms.

Gatovu

The *secteur* of Gatovu is a situated in the *commune* of Ruhashya (see map 2). In 1983, it was comprised of approximately 500 homesteads scattered across two hills. Gatovu borders on the national north-south highway. The majority of brick- and tile-making concerns in Gatovu were very small and operated on government marshland. There was a cooperative, established by the government, which functioned only in name. All these industries specialized in roof tile production[12] while the cooperative in Gatovu, which became effectively defunct during the research period, produced both bricks and tiles on a somewhat larger scale. All of the facilities for brick and tile production were built on the government-controlled marsh and lower-hill slope lands. The tile kilns were the only permanent structures. All of the other structures, sheds, and workstations, were temporary and rebuilt each season. Clay was dug wet from small pits that were interspersed between small agricultural fields (see schema 1). Both the private industries and the cooperative catered to rural peasants or to rural small businesspeople, and sold tiles and bricks in small quantities. In Gatovu, between October 1984 and June 1986 my research assistant and I interviewed 51 people involved in brick and/or tile production in the marsh adjacent to the *secteur*.[13] These informants represented almost all the people involved in brick and tile making in this marsh (3 declined to be interviewed). Eight were employed as workers for others; 1 always worked on his own; 16 usually worked alone, but occasionally hired labor and also occasionally worked for others; 20 fluctuated between working alone and hiring labor; 6 always hired labor and worked in the production process; and 1, a woman, always hired labor and never worked in the production process. None of these brick and roof tile makers were landless; all owned some farmland; all but 3 had access to marshland (government land) for agriculture and 15 also rented lands. All stopped working as soon as the rains started, arguing that they lost too much money during this season if they produced tiles and bricks, and gained more by working their agricultural lands.

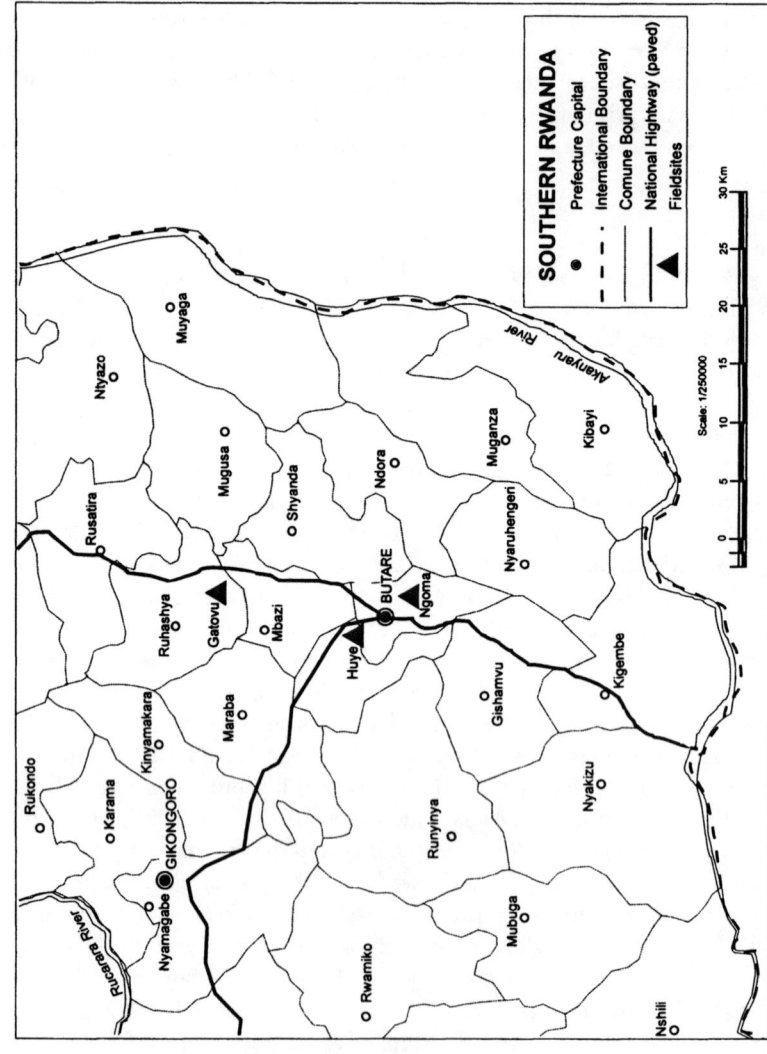

MAP 2. Location of Field Sites in Southern Rwanda

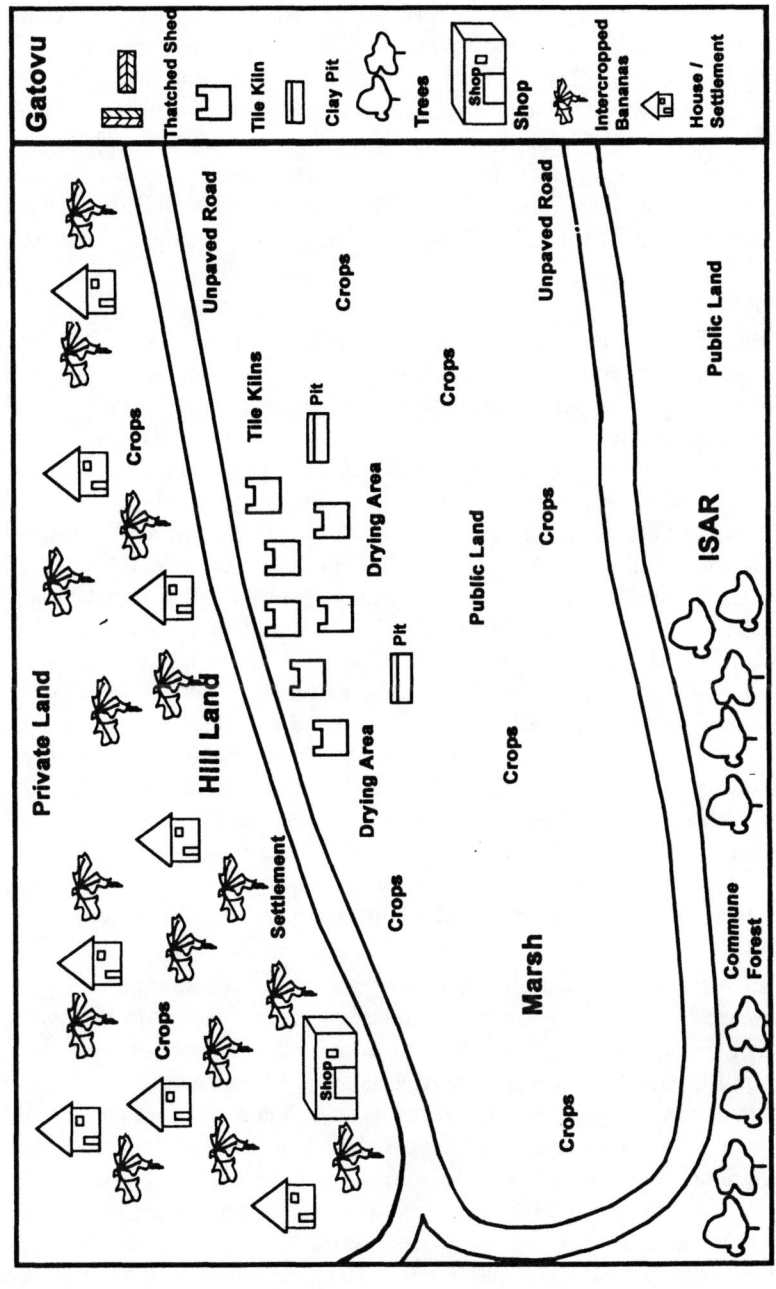

SCHEMA 1. Schema of Gatovu Brickyards and Common Property Land Use

City of Butare: Ngoma and Huye

Between March 1985 and August 1986, my research assistant and I also worked in two marshes adjacent to the city of Butare in Butare *prefecture*. This city of approximately 15,000 is the second largest in the country. It is comprised of two *communes,* the *communes urbaines* of Ngoma and Huye (see map 2). Despite its "urban" status, the majority of the population lived on land they farmed and that provided the larger part of their livelihood. Access to land in these two marshes was very different in 1983, and these differences were reflected in the different scales of the industries and in the nature of the markets they served.

Ngoma. The marsh of Cyarwa-Cyimana in Ngoma is relatively far from a good paved road, and the population resembled that found in Gatovu. The majority living on its peripheries cultivated subsistence crops. The brick- and tile-making industries were mainly small enterprises, principally making roof tiles for a peasant market. Unlike Gatovu, there was one larger-scale brickmaking industry that produced bricks on contract for a nongovernmental organization[14] during the research period (see schema 2). The study centered on the small roof tile makers, most of whom were interviewed. Of the 19 informants, 1 worked completely alone producing unfired tiles, 1 worked only as a laborer for a man who held a monopoly over a portion of the marsh, while 14 habitually shared a workspace with others and fired a kiln with a group, very occasionally working alone, never hiring labor, and rarely working for others, and 1 always hired labor and never worked with his subordinates. Two men alternated between working with others and working for the major entrepreneur in the marsh. As in Gatovu, the workstations were temporary, the tile kilns were small permanent structures, and the clay was dug wet out of small pits found in the agricultural fields in the marsh. All of the men owned land, 10 also had access to agricultural marshlands, and 2 also rented land. None worked in the brick and tile industries in the rainy seasons.

Huye. Nyanza, the marsh in Huye, is situated at the junction of two paved roads, one being the international highway, the other the road to the border town of Cyangugu. On one side is a residential area comprised of expatriates, affluent Rwandans, and government civil servants. On the other side is a small middle-class and poor Rwandan residential area, a jam and juice factory, and two large missions. In 1983, the local population still engaged in considerable agricultural activity on this side of the marsh (see schema 3).

Between 1983 and 1988, there were four private enterprises concentrating on brick production: one employed between 70 and 100 workers, one employed 25 workers, one employed 20 workers, one employed 6 workers, and

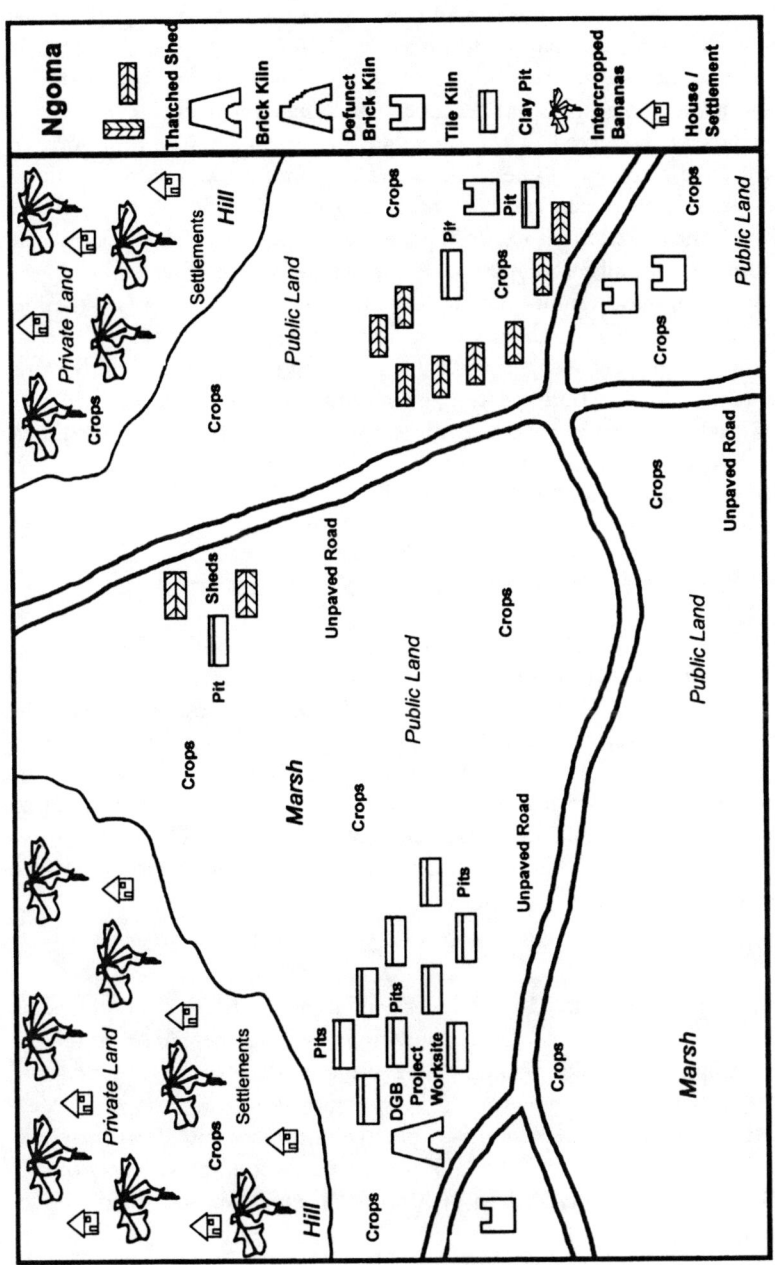

SCHEMA 2. Schema of Ngoma Brickyards and Common Property Land Use

one was a cooperative of 11 persons.[15] In addition, there were two large brickyards, one operated by the prison and one by the Gahinga-Muyaga Catholic Mission. In all, my assistant and I interviewed 36 men who represented only a portion of the brick makers in this marsh, all of whom were associated with the four private enterprises or the cooperative:[16] One was an entrepreneur with 20 employees, 1 worked in the cooperative only, 34 were working or had worked as laborers, 7 of these workers had also once worked with a group as entrepreneurs, and 3 were members of the cooperative. As in the two previous field sites, the workstations were temporary wood and thatch lean-tos and clay was dug out of small rectangular pits; however, unlike the other two sites, the kilns were temporary, built for, and dismantled after, each firing (see the following discussion). The laborers worked only during the dry season, preferring to work on their own agricultural land during the rainy seasons. Because workers were hard to find and keep, most of the entrepreneurs entered into a contractual relationship with the workers who, although they were paid by piecework, negotiated a cash advance. All the workers owned land, 9 had access to marshland, and half rented land.

FIELD SITES IN GISENYI *PREFECTURE*

The two field sites in Gisenyi catered to two urban centers, Gisenyi and Ruhengeri, and to a large commercial agricultural area in Ruhengeri *prefecture* (see map 3). In the 1980s, most of the production was oriented toward the urban market of Gisenyi. Both of these locations are beside the main east-west highway: one on the edges of a large marsh, the other in a valley bottom. Although these sites are approximately 10 km from Gisenyi, they were, at that time, two of the closest brick-producing areas to the city. The research was done in the *secteurs* of Pfunda and Gisa over a three-month period between June and October 1985.

Pfunda

Pfunda is a marsh situated in the *secteur* of Kanama. Most of the marsh is occupied by a government-run tea plantation; however, there are a number of large entrepreneurs making both bricks and tiles in this marsh (see schema 4). In 1985, there were 10 enterprises and 1 functioning cooperative. I interviewed 4 of these entrepreneurs, 5 cooperative members, and 20 workers split between these enterprises. Of the 4 entrepreneurs, 2 employed between 70 and 150 workers, 1 employed up to 30 workers, and 1 worked alone producing unfired products.

The work sites differed dramatically from those in the south. The workstations were built from galvanized iron and wood. Temporary brick kilns

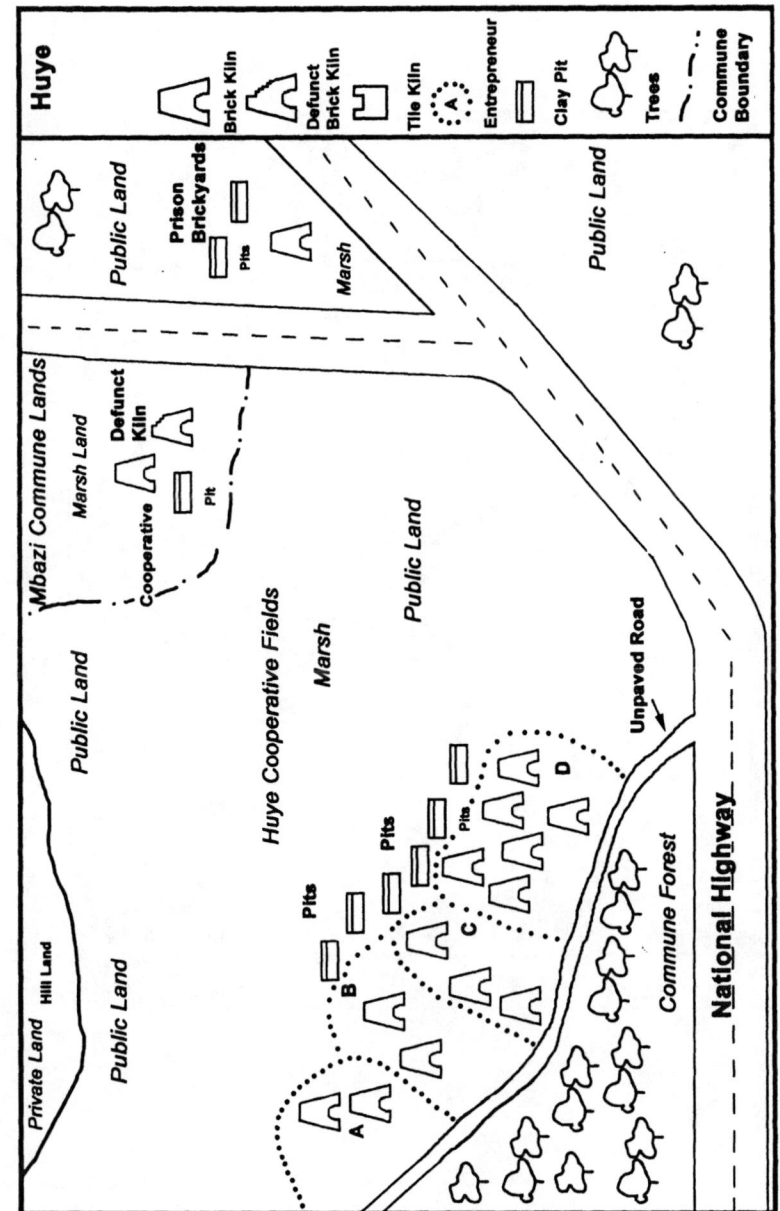

SCHEMA 3. Schema of Huye and Common Property Land Use

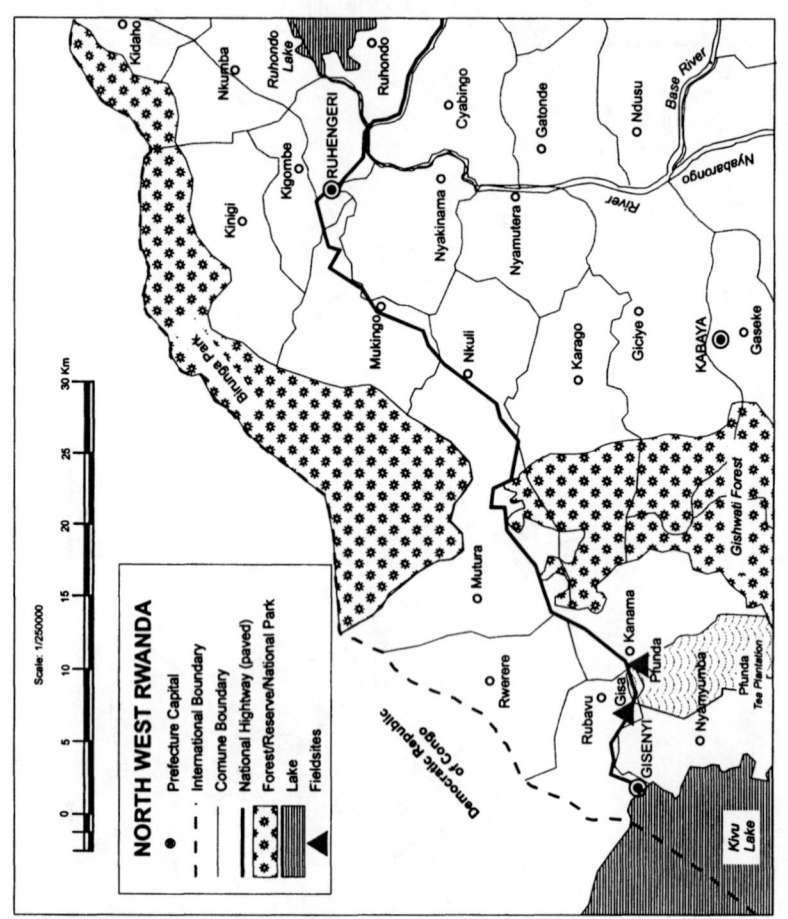

MAP 3. Location of Field Sites in Northwest Rwanda

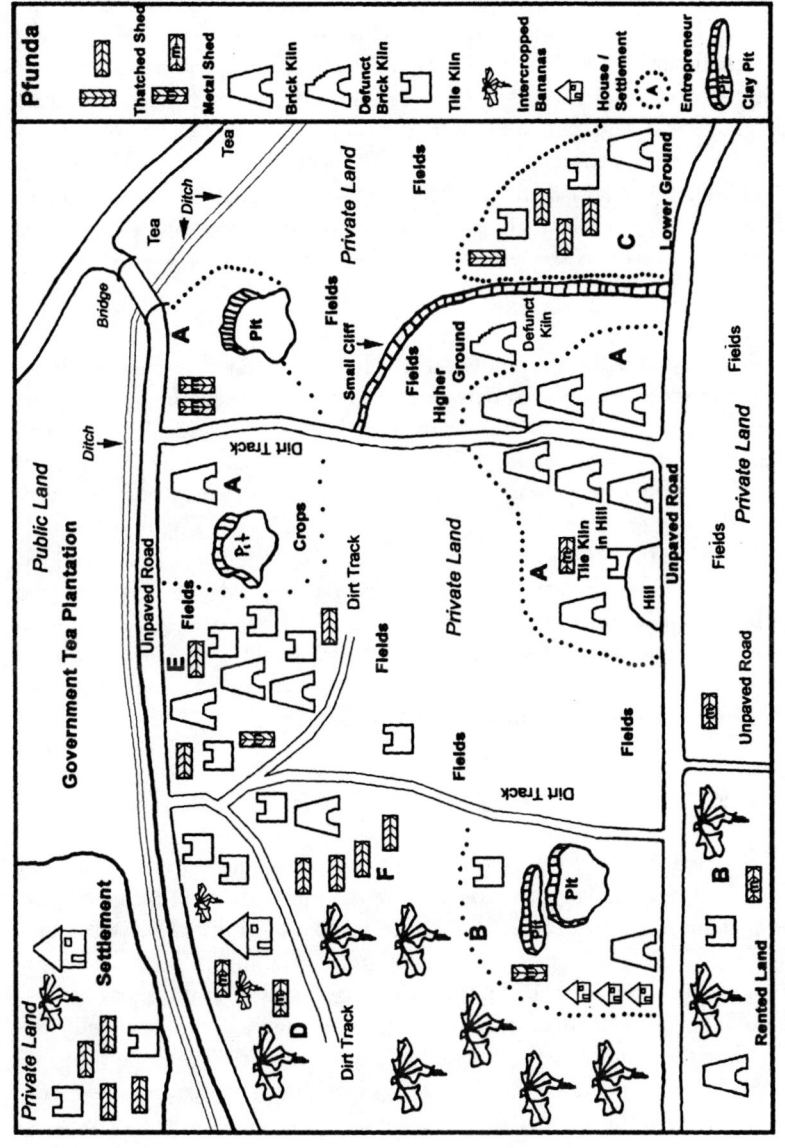

SCHEMA 4. Schema of Pfunda and Common Property Land Use

were built side by side with permanent small adobe tile kilns, and the clay was dug wet out of a large pit at each entrepreneur's brickyard. The 20 workers who were interviewed also differed from those in the south. Most laborers worked as long into the rainy seasons as possible. Two were landless and rented small plots, 14 had very small land holdings, and 16 farmed small land holdings and rented land. Of the 5 cooperative members, 3 described their holdings as small rented land. Despite these small holdings, 88 had to sell staples to meet cash needs,[17] and none grew the major cash crop, coffee, which requires considerable cash inputs. All 4 of the entrepreneurs had sufficient fields and none rented land. These industries ran well into the rainy seasons and restarted as soon as the rains tailed off.

Gisa

Situated in a small valley bottom beside the main highway, Gisa had four large brick industries that employed between 5 and 15 men, depending on the season (see schema 5). All of these industries fired bricks only and all of the owners were absentee, living in either Gisenyi or Kigali, the capital. The laborers all worked as long into the rainy seasons as possible and usually stopped only because the owner stopped paying for the water carriers. These latter were needed because the clay here is dry when dug. All owned small plots of land and 10 rented land. Like the workers in Pfunda they did not grow lucrative cash corps such as coffee. In Pfunda and Gisa, the laborers only worked on a piecework system and only the most trusted could negotiate any cash advances. In both Pfunda and Gisa, the entrepreneurs also engaged night watchmen *(zamu)* to guard the tools and products.

ORGANIZATION OF THE BOOK

The book begins with a description of the technology used in the brick and roof tile industries in Rwanda, considering the most common forms of production technology, clamp kilns and adobe-walled intermittent tile kilns, and the labor processes. It argues that despite great variations in scale, and great differences in economies of scale, the technologies and labor processes used in both the large and the small industries were remarkably homogeneous in the 1980s. Chapter 2 analyzes the nature of labor organization in three forms of industry—small peasant production, large capitalist enterprise, and cooperatives—examining the impact of the regional differences in access to land, labor, and power in shaping labor relations. This chapter shows the bewildering variety of strategies used by these small industries: people working alone, people working in groups, and people selling their labor one season and hiring labor another. All of the large industries used a system of piecework. The

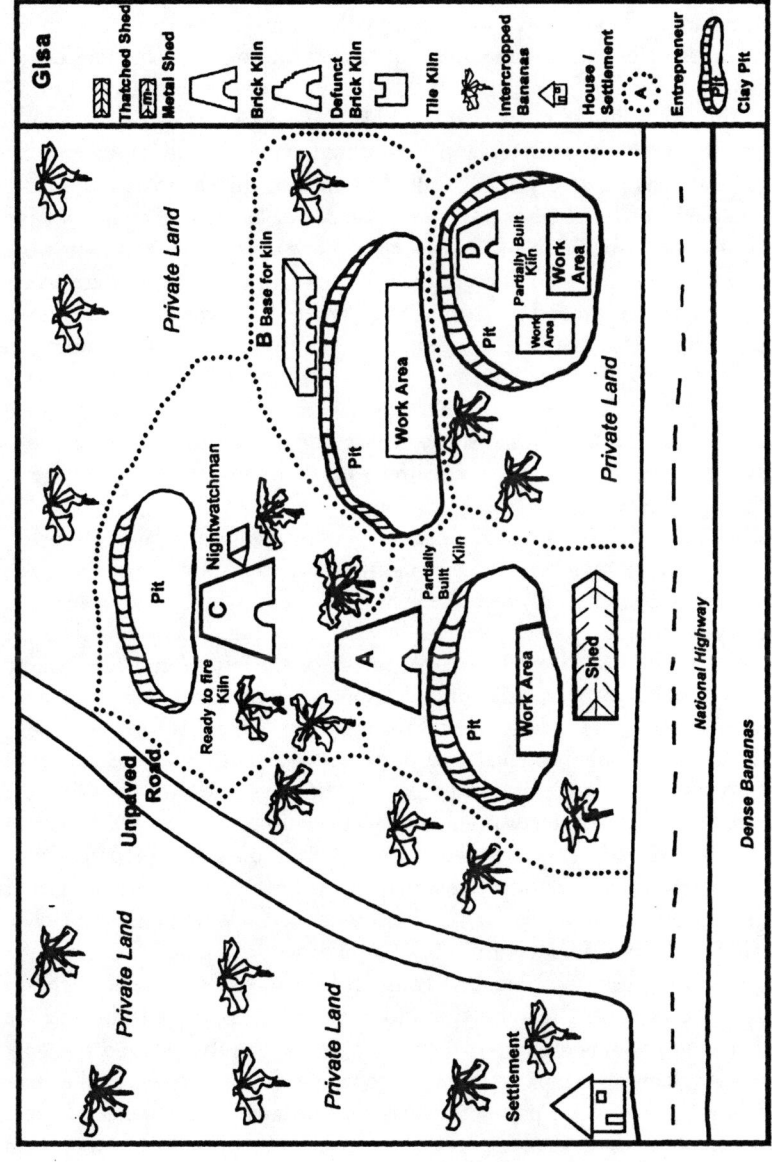

SCHEMA 5. Schema of Gisa and Common Property Land Use

cooperatives were modeled on both systems depending on the scale at which they worked and the region in which they operated. The small peasant-based industries and the capitalist industries were distinguished by the role the owners played in the production process and by their capacity to gain access to the means of production. In these small industries the workers and the owner worked side by side. The capacity of the owner to provide this labor was crucial to the survival of the enterprise. In the 1980s, these industries thrived in areas of universal access to clay land and catered to a poor peasant market that bought products on a very small scale. In contrast, the capitalist enterprises used a system of hired labor paid on a piecework basis. The owners of the enterprise rarely worked in the enterprise and few even supervised their work sites. The large entrepreneurs were most successful in the areas where access to clay land was controlled by clientage and where the owner had preferential access to large urban markets and capital. A number of cooperatives operated side by side with the other industries. Some were organized in a comparable manner to the small enterprises while others were modeled on the large enterprises. This chapter argues that the existence and organization of these cooperatives reflected the nature of government policy and the role of clientage in access to resources.

Chapter 3 maintains that the history of centralization of land, resources, and power; the development of regional diversity; the transformation of the lineage system; gender relations; the recasting of ethnicity in precolonial and colonial Rwanda; and the recasting of these structures in the postcolonial state have profoundly influenced the development of the brick- and tile-making industries in Rwanda and the organization of labor found in Rwanda. It examines the historical development of land tenure, labor relations, and clientage in the precolonial, colonial, and postcolonial periods, and the impact of these processes on land tenure and access to resources, and then considers the ways in which these changes molded gender relations and the role that gender relations played in the reproduction of these industries. Chapter 4 contends that transformation of paternal control over resources and the impact of precolonial and colonial social relations produced a situation in which a household head could not control the labor of grown children. It examines the availability of household labor, and considers the role of subsistence agricultural production in the reproduction of small industries, wage labor, and the household in Rwanda arguing that family members in Rwanda did not necessarily see themselves as undertaking a collective family project. While family labor in brick and tile production was conspicuous by its absence, the role of women's labor in agriculture was crucially important for the reproduction of these enterprises. Women, who rarely owned critical resources, were responsible for household subsistence, while men had the right to control the farm products but did not have to contribute to household subsistence. In almost every case, the small peasant producers and pieceworkers in the study lived in households that produced most of the foodstuffs consumed by the household. Therefore, this chapter also analyzes the development of gender relations in Rwanda and considers the role of women's subsistence agricultural production in the reproduction of labor in these industries. It illustrates the ways in which the surplus produced by women was critical to the operation of the small peasant industries and underwrote the reproduction of the pieceworkers in the larger industries.

Chapter 6 considers the specific cases of three women who have established capitalist brick and tile enterprises, regarding their situation in the light of the literature on class and gender in Africa. It has been suggested that understanding access to critical resources forms a sufficient foundation for analyzing the relationship between class and gender. This chapter argues that the control and use of surplus are equally important and that any analysis of class and gender must encompass all aspects of the social relations of production in a specific historical and cultural context. It highlights the consequences of this history for women and for class relations at both the macro- and microlevels, beginning with the wider context and ending with analysis of specific case studies.

Although many of the specific brick and roof tile industries in this study no longer exist because of the 1994 genocide, the conditions and history that shaped the nature of labor organization and the logic of these industries, coupled with civil war and structural adjustment, molded the politics of genocide in Rwanda. Chapter 7 builds on the analyses of Chapters 1–6 and examines the role of class, regional politics, power, land tenure, and clientage in establishing the circumstances leading to the genocide and in the formation of the postgenocide regime in Rwanda. This chapter shows how these factors led to a situation where when the regime of Habyarimana found itself beleaguered that it turned to ethnic violence as an answer to its problems. It shows how the three conundrums of Rwandan political life fed into a mind-set that made genocide a solution to its political problems. It finishes by demonstrating how the current regime continues to perpetuate the structures that led to genocide.

2

Making Bricks and Roof Tiles in Rwanda
Technology and Process

Between 1983 and 1988, the countryside of Rwanda and the fringes of all the major urban centers were dotted with small and large artisanal brick- and tile-making industries. These provided one of the most important sources of rural nonfarm employment in the country. Because most used the two simplest forms of technology, the clamp brick kilns and the adobe tile kilns, start-up costs were low.[1] The smallest operations were tile-making industries in which all the work was done by one person who shared the firing of a small kiln once during a dry season, while the largest brickyards employed 200 to 300 workers and could produce from 500,000 to 1.5 million bricks a year. Near urban centers like Butare, Gisenyi, Kibungo, and Kigali, the majority of the enterprises produced bricks employing a substantial number of young men. In the countryside, the industries engaged in a mixed brick and roof tile production strategy with tiles being the more important product and source of income. This chapter will begin by describing the technology and labor process used in these industries, and then consider the factors that influenced the differences in scale found across these industries.

The techniques used by the majority of contemporary brick and roof tile industries were introduced into Rwanda at the turn of the century by the first Catholic missionaries in order to build their mission compounds and churches. The German and the Belgian administrations used the same techniques to produce building materials for government construction and housing, a practice that the Rwandan government has continued. During the colonial period, a number of Belgian entrepreneurs ran large brick factories using the same clamp techniques.[2] There were a few cases of Rwandan-run brick- and tile-making businesses before the 1960s but they grew rapidly only in the 1970s.

Between 1983 and 1988, there were three kinds of kiln technology used in Rwanda: intermittent kilns, semicontinuous permanent kilns, and continuous permanent kilns. One type of intermittent kiln, the clamp kiln, and two types of semicontinuous permanent kilns were in common use: the single-chambered tile kilns built of adobe bricks and the multichambered "improved kilns" built of refractory bricks.[3] During this period, the two most important forms of kilns in Rwanda were the clamp kiln and the adobe semicontinuous brick and tile kiln.[3]

INTERMITTENT KILNS

Clamp Kilns

In 1983 there were thousands of clamp kilns in Rwanda and the overwhelming majority of brickmakers were employed in brickyards *(ikilira)* using this technology. These kilns (*itanure*, sing., *amatanure*, pl.) are built out of the bricks to be fired and covered with a mud insulating layer during firing (see fig. 1). The largest kiln of this type in Rwanda fired 300,000 bricks, and the smallest fired 20,000. However, the average clamp kiln in Rwanda fired between 60,000 and 75,000 bricks. The capacity of a kiln is easily calculated by counting the number of fire holes. One hole is built for each group of 20,000 to 25,000 bricks. Most kilns had two or three holes. Labor was organized on a piecework basis, with the employers paying for dried bricks at the time they build the kiln. Employees often provided their own tools and absorbed any losses due to bad weather or breakage before the kiln was ready to fire. The kiln was completely disassembled at the time of sale, and the bricks were stored in the kiln until sale.

Clamp kilns have a number of advantages and disadvantages. The firing process is hard to control and the quality of the finished product is variable, as the United Nations Industrial Development Organization (UNIDO) manual describes:

> The building of a good, tight clamp is an art, but once lit the results depend mainly on the weather, especially the strength and direction of the wind. . . . Although the proportion of first- and second-quality bricks may be increased, . . . underfired bricks are always found at the sides and top where heat losses are greatest, and overfired . . . or even melted together bricks . . . are found in areas of gross overheating. (UNIDO 1969:82–83)

Clamp kilns require little or no investment and have complete flexibility of size; however, fuel consumption is very high (UNIDO 1969:82–83, 100).

FIGURE 1. Loading a Clamp Brick Kiln

Despite the drawbacks to the clamp kiln, a report on appropriate technology argues that "the system has definite potential advantages for some Third World countries, in capital, maintenance and operating costs, and for this reason clamp firing should not be ruled out at any scale of production" (Keddie and Cleghorn 1980:18).

SEMICONTINUOUS PERMANENT KILNS

Adobe Brick Tile Kilns

The adobe tile kilns *(kabuliti)* were the most common type in 1983. These fire a combination of bricks and tiles. The largest capacity kilns fire 10,000 tiles, but the average kiln fires 3,000 to 5,000 tiles. These kilns are usually built by the owner out of sun-dried mud brick; they have straight sides and crenellated tops, and two fire holes at the bottom. All are top loading. Some are built into the side of a hill to make loading and firing more efficient. They usually have two fire holes, the interior walls of which are built from unfired bricks before each firing. The tiles are loaded into the kiln from the top, fired for three days, and cooled for two days, after which the kiln is unloaded. Both the clamp kiln and the tile kiln produce a low-quality product, require a relatively simple level of training and knowledge to operate, and consume a considerable quantity of wood.

"Improved" Kilns

The "improved kilns," as they are known in Rwanda, have four to five chambers, fire approximately 18,000 bricks (and fewer tiles), and use somewhat less wood than the clamp kilns. Firing time is one day. These kilns require a high-quality, well-dried product, and specialized knowledge to load and fire. They need to be emptied after firing and the product stored until sale. Preparation of the clay and drying of the products need to be very carefully done, which increases the cost of the final product. In 1983, tiles fired in small adobe kilns were sold for 3 to 5 FRw[4] per piece, whereas tiles fired in the improved kilns cost 50 FRw per piece.[5] Only specialty bricks (refractory bricks and floor tiling) were commonly produced in these kilns.

The improved kilns were introduced in the late 1970s and early 1980s by development projects (Euro-assistance and Cooperation Suisse) or by the Rwandan government (e.g., the Cooperative Kiln in Gatovu). In a report, two Rwandan researchers pointed out that lack of experience and improper management made these kilns very inefficient (Kamanzi and Rwanga 1986:18). A UNIDO study points out that, while large-scale (i.e., 80 chambers) kilns of this type are almost as efficient as continuous kilns, "small kilns of 5 chambers show a fuel saving of only 15% over intermittent kilns" (UNIDO 1969:86). All of the "improved" kilns in Rwanda in 1983 were five-chambered or smaller. Given that they fire substantially less per load than clamp kilns, and require a large capital cost to establish and specialized knowledge to run profitably, it is not surprising that they were not popular. From their introduction until 1988 when I completed my research, no local entrepreneur had chosen to invest in building this type of kiln.[6]

OTHER KILNS

There were two other types of kilns used in Rwanda between 1983 and 1988, both highly mechanized: the "Chinese" kiln, introduced by a Chinese government project, which fired between 40,000 and 65,000 high-quality bricks a day and was established with a start-up cost of $200,000 (Kamanzi and Rwanga 1986:7–11, 19–20) and the industrial continuous kiln, which only began to operate in 1988. There was only one of each in the country, both in the city of Kigali. Both were beyond the scope of any entrepreneur in Rwanda at the time.

LABOR PROCESS

The two most important kilns used in the 1980s were clamp and adobe brick kilns. The labor process for the production of bricks and tiles for these kilns can be broken down into four stages: winning (digging) the clay; preparing the clay and molding the products; preparing products for firing; and preparing, firing, and drawing the kiln. Within these stages there are a number of production steps that take place, and within the different steps the techniques, tools, and allocation of tasks can vary both by enterprise and by industry. However, whether the production is for a large or small industry, the tools and basic processes in Rwanda are much the same. Tile making requires more skill and more steps in the production process than brick making, and brick making requires more capital. The basic process of brick and tile making in Rwanda uses the simplest skills and tools and the most basic technology.

Winning the Clay. In the initial process of establishing a brick or tile operation, the soil and nonclay layers must be removed and the clay strata exposed. The layers not used in making bricks and tiles are called "overburden" (UNIDO 1969:26). In my field sites the techniques used to prepare the land differed slightly. In Gatovu and in the city of Butare where *commune* land was used, a number of small pits were opened and everyone dug clay from these pits. These pits were allocated for clay digging by the *commune* authorities and were opened by the first users. In these marshes, the clay layer is so close to the surface that there is very little "overburden" beyond the topsoil, which is placed on adjacent fields. None of the pits was very large and the marshland was not severely disturbed or mined out by this process; instead, the marsh consisted of a patchwork of fields and pits. This was the most common pattern of clay digging in Rwanda at the time. In Pfunda and Gisa, where the clay used was found on private land, the pits were very large and very deep, clearly changing the terrain and limiting the amount of agriculture practiced in the vicinity. On a day-to-day basis clearing of the land was done by the brick makers, although unskilled labor was sometimes contracted to clear the initial land cover.

The main tools used are hoes and, if the overburden is moved any distance, buckets and baskets. These hoes are the same type used for agriculture and have a large wide metal blade attached to a long wooden handle by a ring that is an integral part of the blade. The baskets are woven of papyrus rushes or from split bamboo. They are the same type of baskets used for household and agricultural tasks in Rwanda.

On a day-to-day basis, the clay *(ibumba)* used for brick and tile making is dug out *(gakura ibumba)* of the pits with hoes, most often by the brick or tile makers themselves. The clay is found in two forms. Either it is a dry powdery material that needs to be mixed with water or it is a very wet layer found just under the soil in the marshes. In Gatovu, in Ngoma, and in Pfunda, the water table is very high and the clay is dug out very wet. In Gisa, the clay is dry and needs to be pulverized and mixed with water.

Preparing the Clay and Molding the Bricks and Tiles. The clay, brought to the work site, is then prepared for use. The clay is mixed with small quantities of water and beaten with the back of the hoe or kneaded with the feet *(gukaraga ibumba)* until it is the right consistency to be molded. Larger stones, roots, and impurities may be removed during this process. The clay then is usually left to sit overnight. This step is most often done by the person who will mold the bricks and/or tiles, but occasionally someone is paid a fixed sum to prepare the clay. In Gisa, clay was dug as a powder, and mixed with water at the work site. Here too, the mixing and tempering of the clay are most often done by the brick or tile maker. Clay used for tile making needs to be more carefully prepared than that used for brick making because the tile must hold its shape better while drying and, being larger and thinner, when dry can shatter more easily when fired.

Molding the bricks and tiles is done by each worker on a small inclined work surface *(igishyo)* that is attached to a pedestal at waist height. Each worker has their own work area, with the clay to be used placed beside the molding surface. These are built out of flat planks of wood on a waist high pedestal. The pedestals can be built out of various materials: round tree sections; two supporting pieces of wood, one at the top of the surface and one at the bottom; or bricks. The forms or molds *(iforma)* for bricks and tiles are somewhat different, but work on the same principle. Both are made from wood, both are open top and bottom, and both are the depth of the undried product. Brick molds are a square box, 19 cm wide and 6 cm deep, divided into two sections by a piece of wood so that two bricks may be molded at the same time. Tile molds are made from four slats of wood 3 cm by 2 cm in size, and are 25 cm wide at the top and 20 cm wide at the bottom and about 30 cm long and make one tile.

The process of forming is much the same for bricks and tiles. The prepared clay is cut into a lump and this lump is forced into the mold and pounded with the heel of the hand to remove the air bubbles. This action is called *akakirambura* or *ubukarambura ibumba*. It is leveled off with a stick *(umulishyo)* and then moved to the drying area *(imbuga)*. Brick molds then have a flat board slipped under them, while tiles are draped over a handmade wooden paddle *(umubunduro)*, using another handmade wooden paddle *(umuwaruzo)* that is 4cm narrower and scraped with a handmade curved wooden tool *(inkota)* to create a rounded shape.

The bricks are dried until they are ready for the kiln, while tiles require additional shaping and trimming to achieve the required form. The day after the initial period of drying, the tiles, called *umutege* (a tile that is not yet a true tile) at this point, are returned to the worktable and given their final shape. They are placed on the rounded paddle *(umubunduro)* and beaten with a stick *(umusene)* and scraped with the curved tool *(inkota)* until they are smooth. The edges are trimmed to make them even (see fig. 2). The tiles are then allowed to dry again.

Preparing Products for Firing. The drying surface in both cases is a wide flat relatively level area of bare earth. The bricks and tiles are laid out in long rows and left in the sun. When the bricks will hold their shape, they are "hacked," that is, stacked in long rows 6 to 9 bricks high and 2 to 6 bricks deep. These hacks are built so that there is maximum air circulation, with the bricks laid on their sides parallel to each other. Each row is built with the bricks placed at 90 degrees to the last row. The top layers of hacks are often covered with banana leaves to protect the bricks from rain. Tiles are laid out in rows every morning and collected every evening and stored in sheds. These A-frame sheds *(ikibandaholi)* are built on a center pole with a roof made out of banana leaves supported by woven branches.

Preparing, Firing, and Drawing the Kiln. When all the products *(umushinga*[7]*)* are ready for firing they are transported on people's heads to the

FIGURE 2. Trimming a Semidry Tile

kiln or to the site of the kiln, depending on the product and the kiln type to be used. In the case of a clamp kiln, only bricks are fired, and the kiln is built out of the unfired bricks. Each fire hole is laid out on the ground and the bricks are placed in rows to form a flat-topped pyramid with one to twelve fire holes. Tiny spaces are left between each brick (loading the kiln in this manner is called *ubundandi*). The kiln is fired *(gutwika)* with wood fuel. When it is burning well, the whole kiln is "scoved," that is, plastered with a layer of mud. The kiln is fired day and night for six days, then the fire holes are blocked and the kiln is allowed to cool for six days. At this point, the kiln can be broken down, or the bricks (*itafari*, sing. *amatafari*, pl.) can be left until they are sold. Tiles are transported to the kiln and stacked on their sides on top of the fire courses built from unfired bricks inside the permanent kiln. The kiln is fired for three days and then the fire holes are sealed and the top is covered with banana leaves and allowed to cool for two days. The tiles (*itagura*, sing., *amatagura*, pl.) are removed and stacked in the sheds until they are sold.

COMPARISON WITH OTHER ARTISANAL BRICK AND TILE PRODUCERS

The technology and tools used in Rwanda are simple and straightforward, even by the standards of nonmechanized, labor intensive brick and tile industries in other parts of the developing world. The clamp kiln used in Rwanda is the most flexible type of kiln because it exists only as long as it is needed to fire and store the bricks. This form of kiln is comparatively fuel inefficient, but the techniques of using fire holes and daubing with mud, rather than the simplest technique of laying the fuel between the rows, make it more efficient than the most basic form of kiln (Keddie and Cleghorn 1980:18; UNIDO 1969:82–83). The adobe-walled permanent kilns used for firing tiles are a version of the semicontinuous, permanent kiln used in many parts of the world, for example, Mexico and India (Cook 1984:90–107; Cook and Binford 1990; Gulati 1982:37–61).

In other countries, clay preparation is much more elaborate. Frequently there is a more careful selection of clay. Often there are also long periods of weathering of the clay before forming, the addition of fuel and strengthening material, and the use of animal power for kneading (Cook 1984:67–69; Manson 1982:10; UNIDO 1969:42–43). Digging tools such as picks and shovels are more common than hoes; wheel barrows replace baskets and buckets; and molds are often multipartitioned, forming up to twelve bricks at a time, or are simple hand presses. Bricks can either be transported after forming or formed directly on the drying area. The latter produces a more uniform brick (Cook 1984:69–70; Keddie and Cleghorn 1980:15; UNIDO 1969:37–40).

There are endless variations on each stage of production in similar enterprises around the world. Drying can be done directly on the ground or on raised platforms, often under an open shed for protection. Fuels are often a mix of agricultural waste, wood, coal, or peat, but wood is the most common (UNIDO 1969:92). However, in most places, firing amounts to little more than "a bonfire lit beneath a pile of unfired bricks so as to bring them up to a dull red heat" (Keddie and Cleghorn 1980:8).

SCALE OF BRICK AND ROOF TILE PRODUCTION IN RWANDA

There are a number of factors that determine the economies of scale in the brick and roof tile industries: markets, technology, and labor process. The nature of the technology and the market between 1983 and 1988 imposed serious limitations on the tile industry in Rwanda. The adobe kilns hold only 3,000 to 5,000 tiles and need a minimum of 300 bricks to make the internal walls of the fire holes. The alternative technologies do not provide substantial economies of scale and require extensive investments. Such investments are not feasible because the market for tiles is a rural peasant market with limited resources. In the 1980s, most peasants bought only 500 to 3,000 tiles to roof a home and an even smaller number of bricks for gutters and as facing for foundations. With minor repairs, roofs made from these tiles are expected to last the lifetime of the houses (15 to 20 years). Urban markets and wealthy peasants preferred sheet metal roofs or, in the case of the very wealthy, asbestos tile roofs. Bricks were produced for a large-scale, affluent market, rural or urban. Tiles required more skill and labor time to produce than bricks, but the profit (in FRw, not in percentage of return) on a kiln was very low (see table 1). Moreover, the smaller producers in the south who worked beside their workers or who fired a joint kiln with other owners could minimize cash outlay and so make a greater profit than the large producers.[8] The only advantage that large producers in this region had over small producers was the capacity to fire more often and to fill an order more quickly, but advance orders were rare. In addition, the small producer had more flexibility in price,[9] because he did not have the same labor costs, being able to exploit his own labor to save cash. However, as land tenure is more disparate and as clay land access was tied to individual clientage in the north, large entrepreneurs controlled the tile market as well as the brick market. The origins of these disparities and of these tenure systems will be discussed in chapter 3.

Unlike tile making, there are considerable economies of scale to be gained in brick making. Table 1 illustrates the difference: the larger the kiln, the higher the profits. The entrepreneurs in this study considered a kiln of 40,000 the minimum size for a clamp-fired kiln,[10] but kilns this small were rare. On the other end, although only very large entrepreneurs fired a kiln as large as 150,000 bricks, this size kiln was still common. In the clamp-firing process, all the bricks on the outside of the kiln and lining the fire holes are lost and there is additional breakage of the bricks close to the fire or to the surface. The larger the kiln the smaller the percentage lost. My informants calculated that the difference was 10 percent for a large kiln as opposed to 25 percent (or more) for a small kiln. Many of the entrepreneurs fired somewhat smaller loads, because every so often a kiln was badly fired and the whole load was lost. Unlike tile making, smaller brick makers were not in a better position to be competitive than large brick makers, nor were the brick-making cooperatives organized by the government successful. A glance at the figures shows that a small entrepreneur is wiser to invest in a load of tiles rather than in a small load of bricks. Most of the large brick industries in this study fired bricks when they received large orders, had found a market in which they had an advantage because of connections, or because they were in a position to underbid competitors.

The technology used in Rwanda reflected the small amount of capital that most entrepreneurs were prepared or able to invest in these enterprises. Most of the tools were either common farm implements or simply constructed by local artisans or even by the workers themselves. The kilns were the most inexpensive and flexible, and the use of fire holes and scoving reflected an interest in the increased fuel efficiency and brick quality to be gained at minimal expense. The labor process also reflected the small amount of capital that producers were prepared to expend. In the small enterprises, the owners worked side by side with their workers to lower costs, while in the large enterprises the use of piecework minimized expenses for the entrepreneurs, transferring the potential risks and losses inherent in the forming and drying process to the workers. Without a capacity to control access to land, there were no economies of scale inherent in the tile-making process that was limited by the technology used and by the nature of the market for tiles. This was markedly different in brick production. Large-scale production and larger kilns were considerably more efficient, and so economies of scale were important in order for brick production to be profitable. The simplicity of production and the nature of access to land also played an important role in the way in which labor was organized as we will see in chapter 3.

TABLE 1
Comparative Costs of Brick and Roof Tile Production

Task	Tile Kiln (5,000 Tiles, 300 Bricks) Costs	FRw	Large Brick Kiln (150,000 Tiles) Costs	FRw	Small Brick Kiln (40,000 Tiles) Costs	FRw
Winning, preparing, and forming kiln	Winning: 5 man-days @ 100 FRw per day	500	150,000 bricks @ 0.5 FRw per brick	75,000	40,000 bricks @ 0.5 FRw per brick	20,000
	Forming: 5,000 tiles @ 1 FRw per Tile	5,000				
	Forming: 500 bricks @ .5 FRw per brick	150				
Loading and preparing kiln	Transport to Kiln: 5,300 bricks and tiles @ 100 FRw per 1000	530	Transport to Kiln: 150,000 bricks @ 100 per 1000	15,000	Transport to Kiln: 40,000 bricks @ 100 per 1,000	4,000
		0	4 Masons @ 250 FRw per day × 7 days	7,000	1 Mason @ 250 FRw per day × 3 days	750
		0	4 Assistants @ 100 FRw per day × 7 days	2,800	1 Assistant @ 100 FRw per day × 3 days	300
		0	2 Scoving Men (Potapot) @ 100 FRw per day × 1 days	200	Scoving done by Mason and assistant	0
		0	Beer	1,000		0

(continued on next page)

TABLE 1 (continued)

	Tile Kiln (5,000 Tiles, 300 Bricks)		Large Brick Kiln (150,000 Tiles)		Small Brick Kiln (40,000 Tiles)	
Task	Costs	FRw	Costs	FRw	Costs	FRw
Firing	2 Stokers @ 100 FRw per day × 2 days	400	14 Stokers (2 per hole × 7 holes) × 6 days @ 100 FRw per day	8,400	4 Stokers (2 per hole × 2 holes) × 6 days @ 100 FRw per day	2,400
Wood	Wood @ 1 FRw per brick and tile	5,300	1 m⁴ @ 1,000 FRw per 1,200 bricks	125,000	1 m⁴ @ 1,000 FRw per 1,000 bricks	
Unloading	5,300 bricks and tiles @ 100 FRw per 1,000	530	150,000 bricks @ 100 FRw per 1,000	1,500	40,000 bricks @ 100 per 1,000	4,000
Total Costs		12,410		235,900		71,450
Wastage	10% for Tiles = −500 Tiles 25% for Bricks = −75 Bricks		10% = 15,000 bricks		25% = 10,000	
Market Value	4,500 tiles @ 5 FRw = 23,175 225 bricks @ 3 FRw = 675	23,950	135,000 × 3 FRw	405,000	30,000 × 3 FRw	90,000
Profits	93% return	11,540	72% return	405,000	26% return	18,550

3

Making Bricks and Roof Tiles in Rwanda
Labor Organization

A first look at the organization of labor in brick and tile production in Rwanda between 1983 and 1988 showed a perplexing variety of strategies. People worked alone, in groups, or sold their labor one season and hired labor another. By contrast the technology and the labor process used in the large and small industries of Rwanda in the 1980s were remarkably homogeneous despite great variations in scale. The organization of labor in the large capitalist industries differed significantly from that in small peasant industries, and the organization of labor between the small industries varied dramatically. The small peasant industries and the capitalist industries were distinguished by the role the owners played in the production process and by their capacity to gain access to the means of production. In the small peasant industries the laborers and the owner worked side by side in all stages of the operation. Typically, the capacity of the owner to provide this labor was decisive in the capacity of the industry to survive. These industries thrived in areas of universal access to clay land and catered to a poor peasant market that bought products on a very small scale. In the capitalist enterprises there was a separation of property and labor.[1] These latter industries were most successful in the areas where access to clay land was controlled by clientage and where owners had preferential access to large urban markets and capital. Moreover, because of a government initiative, cooperatives operated side by side with the other industries and reflected the nature of government policy and the role of clientage in determining access to resources. This chapter will consider the nature of labor organization in these three forms of industry, examining the impact of regional differences in access to land, labor, and power in forming labor relations.

CAPITALIST ENTERPRISES

Because of economies of scale and the nature of the market, large-scale brick production was most often organized on a capitalist basis, while the tile industries, especially in the south, were dominated by small peasant producers who exploited their own labor to remain competitive. In the southern and the northern field sites, laborers in large capitalist enterprises were paid on a piecework basis, but regional differences in land tenure and access to clay lands affected the relationship between owners and laborers, and determined the extent to which laborers could set the conditions of labor. In the south, entrepreneurs competed for laborers by providing incentives such as advances and individual contracts. They could mount kilns only during the nonagricultural dry seasons because laborers had sufficient land to support themselves in the rainy seasons and invested their labor into their cash crops. In the north, laborers competed for positions and were not able to extract many concessions from owners because laborers did not have sufficient lands to meet their subsistence needs. This also meant that even though the rainy seasons were longer and more intense, many of the northern industries ran into the rainy seasons and laborers continued to work even if it meant bearing losses due to the uncertain weather.

In the three marshes in the study dominated by capitalist enterprises, Pfunda, Gisa, and Huye, there was a clear division between producers and nonproducers. The laborers, in most of the cases, started as laborers and expected to remain laborers, while the owners of the enterprises did not work in any aspect of the manual production of the products. For the most part these enterprises produced bricks, sold in large quantities to merchants, construction firms, or projects on a contract basis. These enterprises were found where there was a ready market, the larger urban centers. Hence, clay land was more highly valued and access was governed by the system of patronage and closed access. These enterprises grew and contracted in scale with changes in the market and in the contracts they were able to acquire.

Despite variation in scale, the capitalist entrepreneurs were all organized on a similar basis. For the most part, they paid the laborers on a piece basis (payment by results). There was a division of labor between three categories of laborer, two skilled and one unskilled. Skilled laborers formed the bricks or tiles, and were also responsible for winning and preparing the clay, and for forming and drying the products. There was another category of skilled laborers who were responsible for building and supervising the firing of the kilns. The unskilled laborers transported the products and did the manual work of firing[2] and drawing the kiln.

Most of the owners of these enterprises were not involved in day-to-day operations. They ran their enterprises as one of a number of other undertakings, such as rental housing, grain dealing, milling, small transportation, shops, bakeries, as well as cash crop production, and often also held good jobs in the government, the military, or in private sector firms. They were considered to be part of a regional and often national elite, and were able to gain access to clay land because of their positions. Most of these enterprises ran when the owner was able to secure an order, using personal connections to win large contracts for government and development sector construction. All of the entrepreneurs in the study had entered into the business with substantial capital and had, at different times, invested capital in acquiring more land and expanding their enterprises. Despite the uniformity of labor organization, the mechanisms used to keep labor varied between the north and the south. Starting with the enterprises in the south, the following section will consider the factors involved in creating this difference and the role played by clientage in the success of these enterprises.

THE SOUTH

There were four large brickyards in Nyanza marsh in the *commune urbaine* of Huye in the south in 1985 when the research was done. Three had been running for a number of years; one had just started up. None had invested in permanent or semipermanent structures; all were organized on the basis of piecework, although some used casual day labor for unskilled work. Of the four, three employed 20 to 30 laborers and one employed over 70 laborers. They dug the clay out of small pits dotted through the marsh; the rest of the marsh was used for small holder agriculture or group agricultural production. The main brick production periods were the dry seasons from June to October and December to January, but the firing period occasionally extended a few weeks into the beginning of the rainy seasons, if they had large orders. Clientage and personal connections played a major role in the success of these businesses.

Two Entrepreneurs of the South: Vianney and Theodomir

The cases of Vianney and Theodomir, show the role of connections in the success of their enterprises.

Born in 1945, Vianney was a doctor working in the local hospital. His wife, born in 1955, worked as a clerk in the university. They had three young children. Vianney had invested in brick making soon after moving to the area in 1979, getting permission through the mayor of the *commune* to use the marshland. He also owned two houses that he rented out to Europeans working in a local project.[3] One was an old house that he had bought in the early 1980s and one was a house he built in 1984, using bricks from his yard.

His enterprise employed between 70 and 100 laborers. When the interviews started, Vianney had two kilns. One just been fired and was being dismantled; the other was ready to fire. Each held 80,000 bricks. Within one week of firing the second kiln, all the bricks were sold. He then put up three kilns of 80,000 each, one small kiln of 60,000, and a large kiln with 140,000 bricks. It took eight men five to seven days to build the 80,000 brick kilns, assisted by boys hired on a daily basis to transport the bricks.[4] It took ten men seven days to stack the 120,000-brick kiln, again using children as brick transporters. All these kilns were built to supply a contractor who was constructing new buildings in the hospital compound. In total the laborers fired 440,000 bricks during a two-month period. For the firing of the big kiln, Vianney had twelve stokers instead of his usual eight.

Vianney came down to the brickyard only on days he did not work in the hospital and left the day-to-day running of his enterprise to a foreman. He established the relations with large contractors that enabled him to sell bricks on this basis. Large contractors were wooed with dinners, bottles of whiskey, and kickbacks. As a doctor, Vianney was in a good position to make these contacts and to gain access to a lucrative contract with the hospital.

Like Vianney, the next entrepreneur, Theodomir, was able to turn his connections, this time with the military and his military income into a successful, albeit smaller-scale, enterprise.

Theodomir, a thirty-four-year-old, ex-military officer who had been in business for three years at the time of the interviews was the only one of the four entrepreneurs in this marsh who was a local man. His family had been moved off their land in 1948 when the city of Butare expanded. They had relocated on the fringes of the marsh where they were able to rent land through kin. He had a Grade six education and had gone into the army at the age of nineteen. His wife had studied at an *ecole familial*[5] and taught sewing and embroidery at the local primary school. When he left the military, he invested his savings and military pension into his enterprise, and used his connections with the military to gain access to clay land.

His business was run on a much smaller scale than that of Vianney. He had twenty-five laborers and two masons working for him, not counting the boys he hired as needed to transport the bricks to the kilns. Most of his laborers also came from neighboring *communes*, and ranged in age from 22 to 45. This enterprise was his major investment and he was always at the work site. His case was unusual in that two of his brothers were his employees. He sold most of his bricks to large commercial firms and to the Catholic mission on a contract basis. He had been able to gain a standing agreement with the mission at the time he began his operation. At the time of the interviews, he was firing two kilns of 80,000 bricks each.

The role of connections for the capacity to mount a successful enterprise cannot be underestimated. Jean-Baptiste, Theodomir's brother, had also tried to start a business with four friends but was not able to retain access to clay land:

> At first we worked for another brick enterprise. With the money we earned we decided to start our own businesses. . . . Four of us worked together, each making his own bricks. We had a contract between us and each put up the money to fire the kiln. . . . Unfortunately it didn't last very long. The big entrepreneurs asked for land in the marsh and they paid a lot extra, so we saw that they had priority. Now I work as a brick maker for a big entrepreneur. I always work on a piecework basis.

The "big entrepreneur" is his brother, Theodomir, who also employs another brother as a laborer. This disparity between brothers was not uncommon in Rwanda, although they did not often work for one another. It was particularly interesting that neither brother was willing to admit to the relationship, which my assistant and I discovered through follow-up interviews with coworkers.

Keeping Labor

In the south, employers more often faced a lack of skilled employees. To maintain a labor force, some owners, like Theodomir, paid out advances:

> I always have laborers available because I pay them to be available. That is to say that we make a contract. I give them an advance of 3500 to 5000 FRw and then the laborer has to work until the advance is reimbursed. Then he continues to work until he has enough bricks to be paid. I always pay them when they want to be paid, no matter when.

He claimed that "I don't have any problems with my laborers and they don't have any problems with me, we are like friends." However, he complained that one of his big problems was "a lack of loyalty" on the part of laborers. The general consensus among the larger entrepreneurs in this area was that one did not give out advances until enough bricks or tiles had been produced to cover the sum.[6]

Occasionally, these entrepreneurs attempted to put off paying until they had sold the bricks, but they were apt to lose employees if they did this too often. Given the mobility of laborers, especially in the south, this was an imprudent practice. Delayed payments were the main reason given by laborers for leaving one employer for another: "I've quit when I've had difficulties with my employers over pay. For the moment I work here with Vianney. Until now he has paid me without causing problems. I don't know how it will be after. I'm happier here in Huye, because in Kigali they often paid us very late, here they pay right after we present our work." However, the stories of other workers in these enterprises made it clear that delayed payments did happen: "I quit the previous two places I worked . . . because there were problems with getting paid," reported one. "We worked on a piecework basis, but we had difficulties with our payments. They always paid us late and we were not happy with him and his 'salary' [rate of pay]," complained another.

THE NORTH

There were fourteen large brick-making businesses in Pfunda and Gisa. Most of the owners held other jobs or had other investments. The enterprises varied in scale between 10 and 300 laborers, firing between 120,000 and 1.5 million bricks a year. Most were brick-making enterprises but a few also made tiles during the rainy seasons. The following two entrepreneurs, Simon and Emmanuel, were typical for these two locations, while the third, Telesphore, was an anomaly who was successful because of his capacity to exploit a niche market. One illustrates the large entrepreneur, while the other illustrates a smaller-scale enterprise.

Three Entrepreneurs of the North: Simon, Emmanuel, and Telesphore

Simon was a functionary in a large intercountry organization based in Gisenyi. He also owned two minibuses that plied a route between Gisenyi and Ruhengeri. He had been making bricks for six years at the time of the interviews. He rented the land on which his enterprise operated; he hired a foreman to oversee the operations and a mason, on a part-time basis, to build the kilns. He had 70 to 100 employees, who worked on a piecework basis forming bricks. These laborers took no part in the loading, unloading, and firing of the kiln. This was done by day laborers. He sold the majority of his bricks to large construction firms in Gisenyi. One of his laborers described the competition in the area, as follows: "Sometimes the buyers come; sometimes the owner looks for buyers. Usually he has to look for them because there are lots of brick makers around here, at Gisa, at Nyamyumba and here. Here the area is vast. One can see how far it stretches. There are at least 10 owners and each is looking to sell." Another said, "Because our boss works at [a large private enterprise] in the city of Gisenyi, he knows a lot of people and that allows him to have lots of clients without much problem." He also ran a smaller tile operation on a year round basis, employing 8 to 10 laborers, 2 of whom worked for Emmanuel during the dry season.

The second owner, Emmanuel, a military officer who lived in Kigali, had hired a foreman, who was also the "mason," to oversee the operation of the yard. He had bought the land in Pfunda on which his enterprise was based. His enterprise, which had 13 employees, ran only during the dry season and he had an arrangement with a much larger entrepreneur, Simon, to employ his regular laborers in a tile operation during the rainy seasons. As a military officer, he had the connections to bid on large projects and was in the process of firing a large kiln (140,000 bricks) at the time of the interviews: "Because there are a lot of others who have the same business, the owner has to do a lot of running to find buyers. It is very rare that the buyers come on their own; if they do it is the friends of the owner who bring them, or it is the friends who come to buy." A laborer emphasized that Emmanuel was able to run this enterprise because "all the materials and the land belong to the boss." His main clients were construction firms and he had been in business two years at the time of the interviews.

The final case, Telesphore, was atypical, as he was the only "self-made man" among all the large entrepreneurs in my study. His success arose out of a capacity to cater to a niche market. Born in 1948, Telesphore came from Uganda and still had his lands there at the time of the interviews. He went from time to time to supervise his parcels there. He stated that he had not sold the land because it had been his father's. In 1973, he bought the parcel of land on which he was now making bricks. He married a local woman in 1975; she had a Grade 2 education and did not engage in wage work. She lived in Uganda and cultivated the fields that Telesphore inherited.

When he first started in 1967, he made a kiln full of bricks and fired them; however he lost this firing because it was not properly fired. He then decided to go to the Nyundo mission to work for the Fathers as a supervisor. He learned his trade there and started his own business after six months. The first four years he worked on his own, firing a kiln every four months. In the beginning, he made more tiles than bricks but, as his business expanded, he made many more bricks than tiles. He was one of the very first brick and tile makers in the marsh in Pfunda. In 1973 he bought the land on which he was working. At the time of his marriage, he stopped making tiles and bricks and moved to Uganda. He returned in 1981 and recommenced his business.[7] At the time of the interviews he had anywhere between ten and seventy laborers working for him depending on his money supply and orders. He worked in the enterprise on a day-to-day basis, supervising the stoking and firing of the kilns.

The scale of his enterprise fluctuated drastically because he did not have a consistent clientele and, as he told us, this meant that "Money is my big problem. If I don't have the cash I can't hire enough laborers to fill a kiln quickly." He produced speciality items that he learned to make in Uganda: round-cornered bricks, bricks with holes used for ventilation, and floor tiles. A number of his special molds were custom-made out of metal. He took special orders and used special molds provided by the customers to fire custom products. He also made ordinary bricks and tiles.

His main customers for bricks were merchants, builders, and development projects; drumming up business was an important part of his work: "I need to go out and find buyers. I go to construction sites to find customers, often I need to 'pay'[bribe] because of the amount of competition." He sold tiles to peasants but stated, "They come themselves and buy. Unfortunately they buy in small quantities, 1000 to 3000 tiles. Bricks are the best because they make the best money, however during slack periods I make tiles because there is always a market." Unlike the market for tiles, success in the brick market was a question of connections. Given his background and the organization of his enterprise, he could be viewed as a very large peasant producer. It was his capacity to see and exploit a niche market that was the basis of his success and expansion into a sizable enterprise. He was the only large entrepreneur in the study to work in his enterprise as a laborer.

Bricks versus Tiles

Tile manufacturing was considered a sideline by the entrepreneurs who manufactured them. Most entrepreneurs did not consider the market worthwhile; however, four out of the sixteen ran tile operations in addition to their brick operations. Two had very large enterprises employing between 70 and 300 people in brick making in the dry seasons and up to 10 in tile making on a year-round basis. Two others had smaller brickyards making both bricks and tiles only during the dry seasons. Tile work was not undertaken by the large entrepreneurs in the south. In the north most marshland was restricted, so there were no sites close to Pfunda where tiles were made by small peasant producers. In the south, the smaller marshes around Huye and Ngoma were the sites of small-scale tile manufacturing. Tile manufacturing was attractive only if there was no competition from small peasant producers.

With the exception of Telesphore, who began his enterprise early and who had specialized in a particular niche market, all the entrepreneurs began on well-capitalized basis. Most invested in enterprises employing more than ten employees. Most of these entrepreneurs bought or rented the land and began making bricks and selling them on a contract basis. Although the size of the enterprises changed with fluctuating markets and availability of contracts, most of the businesses that had lasted had grown steadily larger. The defunct kilns and abandoned sites also bore witness to the failure of a number of enterprises in the same marsh (see schemata 4 and 5 in chapter 1).

THE PIECEWORK SYSTEM AND CAPITALIST ENTERPRISES

In all these enterprises, large or small, north and south, laborers were paid on a piecework basis. Most commonly, each laborer dug his own clay, formed and dried his bricks or tiles, and was paid for these on a piece basis when the kiln was ready to load. There was considerable enthusiasm for this system. Typically, laborers considered piecework a form of "working for themselves," whether they came from Butare: "Voila, this was always how it was: each of us dug the clay, made our bricks and when we had a sufficient number we presented them and got paid. To be precise, each of us worked for ourselves."

from Pfunda: "Each person works for themselves, to present prepared bricks. That is to say each one of us wins clay, prepares clay, forms the bricks in order to be ready to 'show' them when it comes time to fire them. The wages of each person depend on the amount produced."

or from Gisa: "One team draws water, one wins clay, . . . because the clay is about 10 meters from here, and our team is in charge of forming the bricks and presenting them dry for firing, but each of us works for himself."[8]

Most of the laborers in the south saw this system as providing distinct advantages. As a laborer in Butare put it,

> We are paid on the basis of what we present. I find this system not bad because I earn around 350 a day. If I work "per day" I can get only 100 FRw, so you see how much I would lose working for a wage. I even prefer to bargain for the price of the products I will make before I start working. I don't want a daily wage, I wouldn't like it at all.

They saw their income as a "profit" and argued that this system rewarded hard work, as the quotes from the following two laborers show:

> Our "salaries" follow the number of bricks presented, for that reason each of us manages as best we can to work a lot so that we can get more "profits" at the end. We are paid on a piece basis. Myself, I prefer being paid like this because I can make around 700 to 750 bricks which contain about 350 to 375 Frw. This way I can take advantage of the situation to earn money without a lot of bother. That is to say I can work independently and if I want to take a break I can take time off work.

In the south this independence was not illusory. Most men who worked in these enterprises also owned farmland, cultivated by their wives or mothers, grew sufficient staples for home consumption, and grew coffee and bananas as cash crops. Almost all of the men in this region grew some coffee and some bananas for cash. This stands in stark contrast to the workers and farmers in the north who were not able to grow these crops, despite living on better land.[9] Small farmers in the south at this time, appear to have had larger holdings. Because of this situation, these southern workers did not live solely on the wages they earned. This had two effects: the wages did not have to be a "living wage," and if the wages they earned were not satisfactory, they were able to quit and look elsewhere. To attract and keep these laborers, owners had to offer a higher income than agricultural labor would pay and to provide advances. In the north, laborers were far less independent. Most did not have enough land to live on, and to secure cash many were reduced to selling staples or to looking for paid agricultural labor. They rarely grew or sold the higher value coffee for sale nor did they often sell bananas. In contrast to the laborers in the south, more of the laborers in the north expressed a sense of being dependent on the labor they performed in the brickyards and of having only poor options available if they left their work.

In general, the piecework system offered distinct advantages to employers. Most often, the laborers absorbed all the losses and took all the risks until the bricks or tiles were ready for firing. The building and firing of the kiln and the cost of the wood were the major overhead costs, all accrued at the end, because the kiln was built out of the unfired bricks presented by the laborers. One vocal laborer made this very clear: "All the materials and the land belong to the patron. Everyone here works on their own and are paid only when the bricks are dried in the sun. The losses caused by the rain or any other mishap to the bricks not yet presented are the losses of the laborer." Given that, even under the best conditions, 5% losses could be expected when air-drying bricks and 7% to 19% losses for roofing tiles (UNIDO 1969:72, 78) this could be a considerable saving for the employer.

This pattern of transferring risk to the laborer also had a major impact on capital formation, that is to say, on the nature of the investments entrepreneurs were willing to make. Many improvements that would lead to better-quality products or to higher productivity, such as better clay selection and preparation, additives to the clay, and specialized tools, would require an investment earlier in the production process thus entailing sharing risks with the pieceworkers. A number of owners had gone to see new styles of kilns being promoted by the government, but none were interested. They were just too expensive and not very productive, despite small savings in fuel and big increases in quality. All investments in this new technology would take years to pay off. All the permanent kilns needed higher-quality unfired bricks and more infrastructure, and had higher operating costs. The lack of interest in investing in new technology and in improving quality reflected both the nature of risk transfer in these industries and the uncertain environment in which these enterprises operated. The lack of secure tenure over land, even over the land that was ostensibly "owned," and the capacity of the government to drive private enterprises out of business also played an important role. Owners were not willing to invest more than they could recoup in a single firing. The major drawback of the piecework system is the "difficulty of controlling quality when a premium is placed on productivity"(Cook 1984:128). Given that the bricks needed for the majority of buildings did not need to be of high quality, and given this uncertain environment, there was no incentive to change either the technology or the system of payment.

The capacity of pieceworkers to make owners assume some of the risk through salary advances and concessions was dependent on two factors: whether or not laborers could become independent producers, albeit in less desirable sites, and whether or not laborers had sufficient land to be independent financially. Scott Cook contends that "under the piece wage regime, labor is structurally propelled toward self-exploitation . . ." (Cook 1984:124); however, the case of Rwandan laborers shows that the level of self-exploitation was mitigated by social, political, and economic factors and regional differences.

SMALL PEASANT PRODUCERS

The capacity to enter into small, but less lucrative, production and the ability to be agriculturally self-sufficient also strongly influenced labor and investment strategies in the small peasant industries in Rwanda. Unlike the capitalist industries, the small peasant producers used a bewildering number of strategies for labor organization. These fell into four main types. The most common was a mixed strategy of sharing part of the labor process with others, working alone, and working for others. The second most common strategy added the occasional hiring of labor. The third strategy was working alone or with a group only. The final, and most uncommon, was to always hire labor but to also work with the laborers in the production process.[10] The case studies that follow illustrate salient characteristics of these various strategies.

STRATEGY 1: WORKING ALONE, WITH OTHERS, AND FOR OTHERS

The first case is typical of most of the established small peasant producers in Gatovu and Ngoma. However, in Ngoma, most of the producers started by firing the tiles for their homes with a group and then began to produce tiles for the market. Most of these men began tile making just after they had received their inheritance and/or at the time of their marriage.

Gakuzi

Gakuzi was born in 1953; he was married in 1972 and started his tile enterprise in 1975. This man was the son of the hill's traditional healer, who was his father's second wife. He lived in a small round, thatched hut. One of his children showed signs of *kwashiorkor* (protein malnutrition). His eldest half brother had been a "large" tile entrepreneur by the standards of Gatovu, and another half brother was a professor at the University in Butare and lived right beside Gakuzi in one of the only brick homes in Gatovu. Gakuzi had worked at ISAR (Intitut des Sciences Agronomiques de Rwanda, the national agricultural research station) since 1975 as a day laborer in the fields during the wet seasons. He used some of the money he made at ISAR to start his tile business. He and his wife also made and sold baskets to local farmers, and sold coffee, banana beer, and sorghum beer.

Gakuzi described why he began his business and how he learned to make tiles in the following fashion:

> I had problems finding work or even a meal, and I had no other possibilities, so I decided to make bricks and tiles to have something to do and to satisfy my needs. I learned in the marshes, where there were others who knew how to make bricks and tiles. Then I started to work; I always went to the marshes while people were working and watched them. One day I also tried it and succeeded. That was the moment I continued on my own.

Despite his seasonal wage labor and farm income, he frequently had trouble raising enough capital to fire a kiln. "Sometimes if I am lucky," he stated, "clients order and pay me in advance so that I can buy the wood." If he had enough tiles to fill a kiln and enough wood, he fired it himself; if not he split the kiln with someone else. "Very occasionally," he continued," I give credit to good clients but they have to pay me the next time." However, both these situations were rare: "Most often buyers just come down to the marsh and shop around."

He had never been in a position to hire labor, unlike his half brother, Damien (born in 1910), who worked as a laborer in a European firm from 1957 to 1962, and then started his own business. Damien ran his enterprise on a similar strategy to that of Juvenal, discussed in the following section. He fluctuated between working alone, hiring labor, and selling his labor, until he retired in 1980. Gakuzi had never worked with him or for him even though Damien had been one of the first to enter into this business. The strategy used by Damien was typical of older and better-established producers.

Strategy 2: Working Alone, with Others, for Others, and Hiring Labor

Juvenal

Born in 1954, Juvenal had worked in tile production since 1969. He was married and had two children. His wife worked the fields he had inherited from his father when he married in 1979. Most of the crops they grew were staple crops consumed by his household; however, he grew coffee and produced banana beer for sale. Banana beer gave him a steady source of small amounts of cash. Coffee provided a sizable chunk of money once a year.

After finishing Grade 6 at the age of fifteen, he started working by digging clay for pay. During the season in which he dug clay he began to watch the tile makers and soon learned the technique. With the wages he earned digging clay, he was able to buy some wood and fire his tiles with a group who all filled a kiln together, and as he stated, "Like that I started to work for myself." He continued working in this fashion until 1981, when he built a kiln with another man, Augustin: "Most often he made tiles on his own, in the following fashion: First I find the wood. Then I win the clay. After that I form the bricks and tiles. During the next days I come for the drying, and in the end I fire my products. All of this I do by myself." If he had enough money, he fired the kiln on his own; if not he filled and fired it with his friend, Augustin. When he was financially able to, or if he had a large order, he hired a laborer to win clay for him so that he could concentrate on making tiles. Most often he did not work to fill an order. He produced tiles that he hoped to sell in lots of 500 to 1,500 to other peasants who came down to the marsh. When he was not able raise enough money to fire his tiles, he went to work for a short time for others.

Sometimes the change in his fortunes was dictated by the market. When there was a glut of tiles on the market, different entrepreneurs out bid each other either by lowering the price or by offering to pay transportation costs. Every producer had to do this once in a while "so that he would be the one to be lucky and sell his tiles." In this situation he often did not make enough to be able to hire labor or fire on his own. Other times he had an unsuccessful firing and needed to recoup his losses. If he needed money quickly, he worked as a laborer, sometimes on his own and sometimes with a friend, but most often for Innocent, discussed later in this chapter. However, he hired himself out only as a skilled laborer: "When I work as a worker, I only form tiles because the owners prefer that I do it that way so they can have lots of tiles." On the average he earned 400 FRw a day (1 FRw per tile). Innocent estimated that if Juvenal worked with his friend they filled a kiln with a week's work. In that case, Juvenal would earn an average of 2,000 FRw for five days of work. This would give him enough to contribute to the firing of another kiln load of tiles with Augustin.

Over the sixteen-year period he had been in business he had been able to build kilns, but he had never been able to expand his business enough to either stop hiring out his own labor or to be able to hire labor on a consistent basis. Fortunately, his wife's agricultural production made it possible for him to weather his periodic misfortunes. Juvenal had two unmarried brothers who were also in the tile business; one (born in 1963) had set up his own enterprise in 1983, the other (born in 1960) had been working as a laborer for others since 1983. Neither of these brothers had ever worked with him or with each other.

These were the two most common and well-established production strategies in Gatovu and Ngoma. In Gatovu, the men who used the strategy in which they started as laborers, then fluctuated between hiring labor, working for others, and working alone, had been independent producers for an average of 10 years, some as little as 2 years and others as many as 33 years. The men who had been using the strategy of fluctuating between working alone and working with others had been independent producers for an average of 5 years, with some having just started (less than 1 year) and one having lasted as long as 16 years.

In Ngoma, where all but one of the producers fluctuated between working alone and occasionally working for others, the average time that they had produced bricks and tile was 7 years with some operating as little as 2 years and one as many as 16 years. With the exception of the three men who remained laborers, the other five laborers at Gatovu had only worked for others one to three seasons (.5 to 1.5 years). Few of the men who had gone into business on their own had worked more than 2 years, unless they were very young, before they started on their own. For most young men, starting as a laborer was the first step of a career path that allowed them to establish their own enterprise, but for many it never grew beyond working alone or with a group.

STRATEGY 3: WORKING ALONE AND WITH OTHERS

The majority of producers in Gatovu and Ngoma who fluctuated between working by themselves and working with others emphasized their independence, arguing that they worked alone and that even, when they worked in a group, each worked "for himself." Most of the informants described their system in the same way: "I always start by winning the clay, then I prepare it and make the tiles, I do this every day until I put my products into the kiln. The kiln isn't a problem because we always fire it together with the others who work here. We have always worked together in a group, except that each of us works for himself." Most commonly, these groups, ranging from two to five people, were made up of friends. Only one of these informants fired his products with family members, but the strategy was much the same:

> I did everything all alone, that is to say that I dug the clay in the mornings and then I beat it and then I started forming the tiles. The next day I formed tiles again and dried the other tiles until the day I put my products into the kiln. I shared a kiln with my brothers. We used this kiln together. In the beginning, we brought our own wood to see if we could find enough money to continue, but afterwards we weren't able to because the customers didn't come regularly and we didn't have enough money to keep on going, so we decided to leave this business. It didn't last very long.

Generally, this system worked well for most of the producers in Gatovu and Ngoma, allowing them to vary the quantity they produced in proportion to the capital they had available.

There was only one man, in Ngoma, who deliberately worked alone. Born in 1947, he was unmarried and worked alone by choice:

> I've always had the tendency to work alone, from the beginning and up to present, because I don't have the money to pay laborers and also because I don't want to work with others, because they always cause problems. They work irregularly and when there are two of us there are always bad feelings between the two. Normally, I don't fire bricks for sale, I just make enough to allow me to fire my tiles.

One man in Gatovu also worked alone and sold unfired bricks and tiles to those who needed them to top up their kilns. Born in 1955, and still unmarried in the 1980s, he began by digging clay for others in 1972 and then started his own enterprise making unfired tiles the next year. Despite the long years he had worked in the business he was not able to raise enough capital to fire his tiles. When asked why he produced unfired tiles, he answered, "I need to sell unfired tiles because I don't have the money to buy the wood necessary to fire them." His situation was very different from his two brothers. One married brother born in 1954 and one unmarried brother born in 1963 were small tile producers who each fired tiles with a different group. However, he was a surly and unpleasant man who was shunned by the others. Generally, the other producers in the marsh preferred not to sell unfired bricks and tiles if they could raise enough cash to fire a kiln, arguing that "those who have kilns get all the profits."

STRATEGY 4: ALWAYS WORKING WITH HIRED LABOR

Only four entrepreneurs in Gatovu and one in Ngoma were in a position to hire labor on a consistent basis. Of these, three in Gatovu worked beside their laborers,[11] as in the following case.

Innocent

Born in 1938, Innocent was one of the most affluent tile producers in Gatovu. He was married in 1960, and had ten children. He grew and sold bananas, banana beer, sorghum beer, and coffee. He began with the money he raised through these sales. Innocent always hired labor. He had never bothered to learn how to make bricks or tiles. Because he had the capital, he could hire skilled laborers to do the actual forming of the tiles. However, he did the heavy unskilled manual work associated with the production process himself (the winning and preparing of clay and the firing and drawing of the kiln). He described his system as follows: "I dig the clay and beat it and then I must go and look for laborers. If the work is not too urgent, I hire one; if it is urgent I hire two, usually Juvenal and his friend, Emile, and one man to fill the kiln and we work for 5 days to make enough to fire a kiln." When he could, he bought unfired tiles and fired them and sold them. He did this when people were willing to sell unfired products. He argued, "I prefer this system (buying unfired tiles), because it is cheaper." However there was only one man who was willing to sell him unfired products; most tried to fire the products themselves.

Like the other entrepreneurs, Innocent sold his bricks and tiles to peasants. Sometimes he offered credit; other times he lowered the price of his goods: "Because there are lots of people who want to sell their products, I don't have a fixed price. I always bargain for the price with my customers."

Innocent had one brother and two half-brothers who independently made bricks and tiles. Two, one brother born in 1945 and one half-brother born in 1958 fluctuated between working on their own and hiring some labor. These men worked side by side with their employees making tiles and bricks, like Innocent. The third, a half brother born in 1954, worked the same way as Juvenal, fluctuating between working alone, working for others, working with others, and hiring labor. None of these four brothers had ever worked for or with each other.

There were two other owners in the marsh who ran enterprises in the same way. One was a young unmarried man, born in 1959, who began his enterprise in 1979 when he received his inheritance; the other was a married man, born in 1945, who began his enterprise in 1970. Neither of these two men had worked elsewhere; rather they had invested their agricultural income from their lands because they considered tile making to be a lucrative source of income. Like Innocent, they were among the more affluent agriculturalists in the *secteur*. Each of these men had a younger brother who had worked for them for one season and then set up an independent business on the model of Juvenal's (Strategy 2) or Gakuzi's (Strategy 1) enterprises.

Open access to clay land and the simple technology allowed the men in Gatovu and Ngoma to easily fluctuate between being laborers to running small enterprises. These factors also made it difficult to maintain control over a pool of cheap labor. Due to the lack of economies of scale in the technology and the nature of the tile market these enterprises ran at a very low level. For the majority of producers, the reproduction of their labor through women's work in agriculture made these fluctuating production strategies viable. All but the last of these factors combined to limit the potential for the transformation of the larger enterprises into capitalist industries.

The three larger-scale entrepreneurs, who always worked with hired labor, were able to remain in business because they sold to a somewhat wider clientele and could produce quickly, thereby increasing the rate of circulation of capital. They produced somewhat more bricks than the others and sold bricks and tiles to the local merchants in the small commercial centers nearby and to ISAR. They either owned wood lots and/or had connections with the *commune* and with ISAR that allowed them access to cheap wood. These three men minimized their costs and maximized their profits either by buying ready-to-fire products or by doing the unskilled work in the production process. They preferred to pay highly skilled laborers the going rate, while reducing expenses by preparing the clay themselves. This strategy served two purposes: it was faster and produced a larger number of tiles in a shorter time, and it insured a better-quality product.[12] However, because of open access to clay land and the small scale nature of the peasant market, they were not able to expand their enterprises into capitalist industries. The final form of brick and tile making found in the field sites was the cooperative.

UNCOOPERATIVE COOPERATIVES

There were five cooperatives in the field sites studied. Brick- and tile-making cooperatives were a short-lived experiment in Gatovu, and had taken on an unusual character in the other areas. In the open access marshes, such as Gatovu and Ngoma, the cooperatives were created arbitrarily by local government authorities, causing complications for many of the producers. In Gatovu, thirty of the thirty-nine cooperative members stated that they were forced to join the cooperative:

It was the mayor of the *commune* who saw that there were people making bricks and tiles privately and decided to start a cooperative. He saw that the brick and tilemakers made a personal profit, but he thought that it would also be good for them, and for the *commune*, to start a cooperative. Since then we started a cooperative.

This was not a popular move. On one of our first visits to the field site, my assistant and I met with a group of men, and began to discuss brick and tile making. The mood is best caught in the fieldnotes of my assistant: "We found some people and asked them how they worked, if they worked for themselves or not. They told us that it was a cooperative and that they worked for a cooperative but it wasn't their idea" (Beatrice Ntabomvura, October 6, 1984). Two thirds of these men were between 35 and 50, but a new policy was initiated soon after the cooperative was established: "We had just fired our last kiln which was very large, we had lots of money . . . and this was when the mayor and the official responsible for the formation of cooperatives came to tell us that the cooperative was to be only for the young." Many of the men were relieved to be able to disassociate themselves from the cooperative, however, most men stated that they were "temporarily" working for themselves, while still being cooperative members so as to avoid potential trouble with local authorities.

The cooperative in Gatovu was very unpopular because it had constant financial and organizational problems. There was a major reorganization in 1985. The majority of the complaints about this cooperative hinged on the failure to distribute funds. The members felt that the funds had disappeared and that they had worked for nothing: "Our money has disappeared and no one can answer why," stated one. Others quit because they had put in long hours but did not make any money. One argued, "I didn't like working for the cooperative because I found that my family's resources dwindled because I was always working there." Another declared, "The co-op could force us to work any time, and that season [1984] we worked every day. I found that there were no benefits to be gained by working in the co-op and that there was a lack of sociability in the co-op and in the work." The president of the cooperative and the other members of the executive were most commonly blamed for this situation:

> We have never redistributed the profit because the accountant and the president lost a lot, so we haven't had any money to divide and so we decided to quit, because there is no point in working for nothing. I have decided to work for myself because it is more profitable and more advantageous for myself and my family.

The president and the other members of the executive on the other hand, gave me elaborate accounts of the different systems by which they redistributed the profits, or all the reasons why they did not. The ex-president, who was in the process of building a large new house during the interviews, defended his actions, arguing that "We never split the profit because I had a plan to save up to buy a pick-up truck. The members did not accept my advice. They were suspicious of me. They did not understand me and reproached me for starting the cooperative so I decided to quit." His half brother who, at the time was still a member of the cooperative and held a position with the new executive that had ousted the old executive, stated that "There used to be 36 members, but 16 quit so now there are only 20 members. They quit because our budget was lost by our authorities." The fact remained that most of the members saw little benefit to be had from the cooperative and eventually quit.[13] Where small peasant producers already had access to the means of production, the cooperative legislation was seen as an exploitative imposition that threatened their access to clay land. It was resisted in the usual manner of peasants everywhere, acquiescing in word but not in deed.

The second "cooperative" was in the north. It was a cooperative in name only and was clearly used to get access to land. It was run by two men who were related. This was a small enterprise in which the two men pooled their resources, hired labor, and made tiles. Started in 1979, it continued until 1985 when the informant's uncle died. Jean-Damien explained,

> We work along side the workers we have hired, who "present" dry tiles ready to be fired. My associate and myself take care of the firing, because it is our land and our drying shed. We split the profit equally between us after paying the workers. The biggest problems we have are finding wood and finding a truck for transporting it. I've never quit my cooperative, except it has been stopped for the last 3 months due to the death of my associate. I'm hoping to restart in a few days with his son.

Of all the enterprises surveyed in the north, this was the only one in which the laborers and the owners worked together. Structurally, it was indistinguishable from the more successful peasant enterprises in the south. The owners' claim to being a cooperative was effectively a ruse to obtain control over clay land in the marsh.

The cooperative in Pfunda in the north was even more intriguing. This cooperative had been operating since 1976, a full nine years at the time of the interviews. They had begun using a classic cooperative model, but found it did not work. One member explained the two systems in detail:

> Before we worked in teams, one team of 2 water carriers who also won the clay, one team of 2 who prepared the clay, and one team of

3 who formed the tiles. At the moment each person does the whole job himself. We did this because often the production of different members was different and some worked harder than others. That's why we reorganized the system and each person gets out of it what he puts in. At one time we each got an equal share of the profits, nowadays we each get the amount of money due us for the tiles we make. We don't have enough money for keeping up a kiln, so we prefer to sell our tiles unfired and the buyers fire them. A sun-dried tile costs between 1 and 1.5 FRw. The other entrepreneurs who make tiles in the valley often come and ask us to sell our products to them. Any one of us can sell our products because we count the number of tiles each of us makes.

Another elaborated on the problems that they had had: "Before we used to produce and sell together, then we had a system of a minimum number, now each one of us sells what he produces. The production of each person was not the same. We didn't have a kiln. We had problems with negligence and with absences. Now we all work for ourselves." This last man's brother had doubts if they could really be called a cooperative:

Today each of us works for ourselves. Each carries his own water, wins his own clay, forms his own bricks and sells his own products. We are workers for ourselves. Anyone can sell the tiles but they must give the money to the person who made the tiles. I've never quit the cooperative, but today we each work for ourselves, so I'm not sure you can call it a cooperative any more.

However, despite the fact that they worked in a group, they were unable to raise the cash to fire a kiln. Wood was much harder to get in this area, so most of the large producers hired a truck and hauled it a long distance. These small producers would have found this arrangement very expensive, given the scale of their production. This cooperative ran very successfully, much like the "groups" of single producers found in the south.[14] However, given the land tenure system in the north, they would have found it difficult to get access to land without calling themselves a "cooperative." In Huye and in the restricted access section of Ngoma, both in the south, which have been largely monopolized by capitalist enterprises, there were two similar cooperatives.

Organizing a cooperative was one way for these groups to gain access to marshland in lucrative areas that had closed access. When strategy was combined with the customary way of working it seemed to be successful. It was very clear that, in the marshes where the large capitalist enterprises had a monopoly on the clay land, the cooperatives seemed to exist mainly so that the *commune* authorities could meet the letter of legislation from higher levels of government requiring that cooperatives be organized. Ironically, their strategy did not differ from that used by most peasants who saw themselves as independent entrepreneurs.

Despite the inability of most of these cooperatives to work as a group and to share the profits, there were cases in which informal groups were able to make this type of structure work. One such was the case is described by a laborer who had worked with such a team:

> We numbered 12 people who worked for one entrepreneur in Kigali. We always made a contract with him for a full kiln that held 120,000 bricks, for 60,000 FRw. That is to say, when we made the bricks for 0.5 FRw each. It was the other workers who transported the bricks to the kiln and the masons who loaded the kiln, which is their work, to build it. The other costs like lodging, food and other luxuries, were our responsibility and not our boss' responsibility.
>
> In Ruhengeri we worked like we did in Kigali, but we also did the work of firing the kiln. That is to say, the money was higher. Not only that, because we were far from home and asked to come, he paid us more than in Kigali. For a kiln of 120,000 bricks he gave us 72,000 FRw, for a full kiln ready to fire. That means that we did the work of making the bricks and building the kiln for this amount. After the kiln was built he hired us to fire the kiln and guard the kiln during the firing. For these things we made another contract. One kiln of 120,000 bricks contained around 15,000 to 20,000 FRw for the whole of the firing. That is to say, for one kiln of 10 fire holes he paid us 15,000 and for one of 12 fire holes he paid us 20,000 FRw. A 10–hole kiln took 5 to 6 days to fire, so you can see that the money was not as interesting, except that it was better for those watching the fire, they were paid for one night or one day. This arrangement pleased us a lot because we earned a lot of money and our boss was happy too.

In fact, the boss in Ruhengeri paid slightly more per brick than he would have by hiring the laborers individually, 0.725 FRw as opposed to 0.766 FRw, but the whole group supervised itself and guaranteed the quality of the product, which probably saved him money in the long run. However, they were able to sustain this group for only one season and this informant had gone back to working independently for a large entrepreneur.

MAKING BRICKS AND ROOF TILES IN RWANDA

Big or small, peasant or capitalist, all Rwandan brick and tile industries used much the same technology. Tools were common agricultural tools, or could be made by the laborer or by a local carpenter. The clay was used almost in the condition in which it was found. Forming techniques were learned quickly, without any formal training or apprenticeship. Although the technology was appropriate for local conditions, there were still many small technical improvements that could have enhanced the efficiency of labor and the quality of the final product. However, the owners in my study were either not interested in, or not in a position to, implement the majority of these improvements. Both the nature of labor organization and the technology allowed employers to minimize risk and investment.

In all the field sites, payment was on a piecework basis or jobs were contracted out. All the stages of brick and roof tile production were done by men and most enterprises in Rwanda were headed by men.[15] Men virtually never used family labor in these enterprises and hired labor when they wished to expand their production. The system of piecework that transferred risk to laborers, the lack of secure access to productive resources, and the small investments needed to initiate the enterprises have influenced the nature of the technology adopted by these enterprises. The critical factor determining the capacity to mount a large brick-making enterprise was access to good clay land situated near a good road and a large market. Artisanal brick- and tile-making industries were primarily situated in the marshes, valley bottoms, or on lower slopes. This form of land was controlled by politicians, so access to clay land and clientage were inextricably intertwined. However, the ways in which this phenomenon affected the scale of enterprises differed by *commune* and differed drastically between the north and the south. In some southern *communes*, such as Ruhashya, and in rural parts of Ngoma and Huye, marsh and valley bottom land was parceled out to a large number of families by *commune* authorities. In others, such as the urban areas of Huye, access was restricted to a small number of large entrepreneurs. All such land was considered to be public land. In the case of the north, in Gisa all the valley bottomland was privately held, while the marsh around Pfunda showed a mixed ownership. It was the site of a government tea plantation, but the brick makers were found on the "privately owned" edges of this marsh. However, tenure over land in all these areas was not secure, though the extent of land security varied with the land use and land distribution patterns in the various marshes.

From 1983 to1988, marshes far from lucrative markets tended to be open to a larger range of men. This openness favored the development of small peasant production in these locations. Marshes in favorable locations were allocated on a patronage basis to individuals in a position to mount large enterprises. In these marshes, the capacity of such men to control access to land favored the development of capitalist enterprises and excluded small peasant producers. In the rural or less-favorably placed marshes the dominant pattern of land use was one of small agricultural holdings planted in seasonal crops such as sweet potatoes, sorghum, and beans. Small plots were widely distributed and the right to use this land was closely monitored by the *commune*. The right to dig clay was allocated to all the members of the *secteur* and the pattern of clay digging was specified. Cooperatives worked only when labor was organized in the same way as in the local enterprises, either like the small peasant groups that produced individually and fired cooperatively, or as a small enterprise in which the owner worked beside the hired laborers. Forming a cooperative was primarily a strategy for obtaining access to state-controlled public lands. Regional differences, systems for allocating clay lands, the different patterns of land tenure, and the nature of labor relations are rooted in the history of Rwanda. As we will see in chapters 4 to 7 these factors were also important in setting the preconditions for the genocide.

4

Land Tenure, Common Property, and Labor and Power

Precolonial, Colonial, and Postcolonial Transformations

The regional, class, and political differences; the gender and household relations; and the land tenure systems that shaped the brick and roof tile industries are rooted in the development of the Rwandan state and ethnicity. The nature and history of the precolonial state, and the origin and meaning of ethnicity in Rwanda, however, all have been topics of debate since the first European arrived in the region. Not only have these debates occupied Western academics and administrators, but the interpretation of history and of the meaning of ethnicity have also been hotly debated by Rwandans. For the people living in the region these controversies have had serious consequences. Different interpretations of ethnicity and statehood have been used to create and justify policies of exclusion and inclusion, and claims to legitimacy from the colonial period to the present day.[1] There are competing and often diametrically opposed interpretations of history and events between groups, each demanding that observers validate their views and negate all other views. This debate takes place through emphasis and omission, through the writing and rewriting of events. The further back in time the discussion goes, the more speculative the analysis and the more open to the manipulation of allegory, myth, and legend. The period just before colonialism is better substantiated than earlier periods, and colonial and postcolonial periods are the best documented.

Conquest and colonialism, both indigenous and European, have played a critical role in the formation of the modern Rwandan state and the centralization of land, labor, and power into the hands of a tiny elite; the level of exploitation or equity in this system has been hotly debated. Beginning in the precolonial period, intensifying and transmuting under the Belgian colonial period, undergoing further transformation under the First and Second republics and altering again under the current government, the rewriting of history has been a major academic and political project in Rwanda. Central to this project have been the characterization of the nature of precolonial rule, and the role played by various ethnic groups in the precolonial state.

PRECOLONIAL RWANDA

Early Rwandan History

There is no shortage of writings on the precolonial state, both within and outside Rwanda, but there is little agreement about the nature of that state. Authors such as the Abbé Alexis Kagame (1972); Jacques J. Maquet (1961a, 1961b, 1967, 1969); L. Mair (1961); Gravel (1965, 1968b, 1968a); and even Jan Vansina (1963) see the Rwandan state as an equitable, albeit somewhat hierarchical, state, contending that the clientage system, while unequal, was based on reciprocity and offered considerable benefits to the clients. On the basis of this material, Basil Davidson tells us,

> Ruanda . . . was the postcolonial descendant of an old kingship in these pleasant uplands along the southern reach of the East African Rift. The general 19th century move toward more emphatic forms of centralised power had developed the dominance of a minority group, the Tutsi, over a Hutu majority. But the manner of this 19th century dominance was mild, and was regulated by "lord and vassal" relationships which had some resemblance to the simpler forms of European feudalism. "The rich man in his castle and the poor man at his gate" appear to have been the outward and visible forms of a mutually acceptable relationship between Tutsi and Hutu; at least in principle these forms represented an agreed sharing of rights and duties. Colonial enclosure changed all that. (Davidson 1992:249)

In contrast, some powerful proponents in the Rwandan scholarly community, most notably Ferdinand Nahimana (1987), emphasize the exploitative nature of the precolonial state and the role of the Tutsi in this state and see the Tutsi as an "outsider" group. Starting from the premise that the Tutsi are invaders and that the Hutu are the "natural inhabitants" of the land, this work seeks to discredit the right of Tutsi to rule or even to inhabit Rwanda. This rewriting of the "Hamitic hypothesis," the idea that the Tutsi are a separate racial group coming from Ethiopia who invaded Rwanda, formed the basis for the appalling propaganda of the "Hutu Power" extremists of the last regime, of whom Nahimana became one of the most virulent. This perspective has been well documented by Jean-Pierre Chrétien and the Reporters Sans Frontières (1995).

These diametrically opposed views overlook the work done by both Rwandan and Western scholars from the 1960s until the present day, which shows the complex and changing nature of the precolonial kingdom (Des Forges, 1972; Lemarchand 1994a; Meschy 1974; C. Newbury 1974, 1978, 1980, 1983, 1988; D. Newbury 1980a, 1981, 1987, 1995a; Rwabukumba and Mudandagizi 1974; Vidal 1969, 1974, 1984, 1985, 1991). The debate, over whether the precolonial state was equitable or exploitative, can be considered to be a "metaconflict," that is to say, a conflict about the nature of the conflict. René Lemarchand, who has coined this phrase to describe the same debate in Burundi, tells us that "It is one thing for a reasonably dispassionate observer to try and assess the roots of the Hutu-Tutsi problem; but how members of each community perceive their predicament, what each attempts to suppress as well as invent, is an altogether different matter" (Lemarchand 1994a:17). Instead the political actors involved in the conflict in Burundi each connect

> past and present through divergent paths. No attempt to demystify the Burundi situation can fail to appreciate the chasm that separates the reality of ethnic conflict from the manner in which it is perceived, explained and mythologized by the participants. Reduced to its essentials, the conflict about the Hutu-Tutsi conflict revolves around 3 basic disagreements: the significance of ethnicity as a source of tension; the nature of cultural differentiation between Hutu and Tutsi; and the role of history in shaping ethnic antagonisms. (Lemarchand 1994:17)

The same is true for Rwanda. Although Rwanda and Burundi approach the current problems they face through different historical paths, their intertwined current histories mean that the "metaconflict," the conflict about the nature of the conflict, has ended up being phrased in similar terms.

When we turn to the recent historical, political, geographic, and anthropological work done on precolonial Rwanda, we find a "history" far more complex than the competing characterizations of the Rwandan state would have us believe. The image of "mild dominance" in the precolonial kingdom is shattered by the turbulent transformation of land, labor, and power relations. Similarly, Davidson's bland "move towards more emphatic forms of centralized power" (Davidson 1992:249) becomes a longer and more violent process through which land and power are centralized into the hands of a tiny aristocratic elite.

The Rwandan kingdom that Europeans encountered in the late nineteenth century appears to have been created by a pastoralist clan, the Nyiginya, and their armies, who moved from the area of what is now eastern Rwanda into the preexisting agriculturalist and pastoralist kingdoms to the west, north, southwest, and northwest, through a long process of conquest and assimilation. It seems that the original Tutsi kingdom was modeled on these agricultural states, in which kings *(baami,* or *bahinzi)* had a sacred function and only minimal political or economic control (Des Forges 1972; D. Newbury 1987; Rennie 1972; Vansina 1962). Whether these pastoralists represent a different racial/linguistic group or not has been a major controversy in Rwanda. Most commonly, in this debate, the Tutsi are characterized as either being Nilotic, members of a different linguistic group associated with pastoralists in the Horn of Africa, and East and Central Africa, or being Hamitic, a different racial group considered by European colonists to be descended from European or Middle Eastern origins (Lemarchand 1999:8; Reader 1997:308–309). European colonialism justified favoring the "Tutsi" over the "Hutu" on the basis that the pastoralists were a different "race." The people called Tutsi speak the same language, Kinyarwanda, a Bantu language;[2] practice the same religion; live intermingled and intermarried throughout Rwanda; and show far more phenotypic and cultural variation within the group than between Tutsi and other groups. This arcane debate has become important because of the power these ideas have been given in the political debates in this century, but sheds virtually no light on the origins of the phenotypic difference found in the extremes of the ethnic groups.

The core of the current Rwandan state seems to have been established by Ndahiro Ruyange.[3] Judging from oral history accounts and from material from the peripheries of the Rwandan state, the most important political units were lineages and neighborhood groups, and the main powers were vested in the hands of the lineage heads (C. Newbury 1988). Among the agricultural groups, these heads distributed land within the lineage and granted land to individuals who demanded it. These clients of the lineage *(abagererwa)* had an obligation to provide gifts of food or beer to the lineage in return for the *use* of land. The land continued to belong to the lineage and could be withdrawn by the lineage. Clients could marry into the lineage and so become members (Des Forges 1972:2; Rennie 1972:16; Vansina 1962:60–62). The frontiers of this kingdom appear to have been expanded by settlement in newly pioneered land and by conquest (Rennie 1972:16). However this state differed from its neighbors in that it established "a continuing, strongly centralized political organization with institutions which incorporated both pastoralists and agriculturalists" (Rennie 1972:25).

Kigeri Mukobanya appears to have enlarged the ceremonial and real powers of the king *(mwami)* and established a permanent military organization.

He is credited with forming the *ntore,* "small armies," and organized them into *ngabo,* "larger armies," based on lineages. Power appears to have been based on control of men and not control of land. War chiefs exacted tribute *(ikoro)* from the regions they controlled, and, although they sent a share of this tribute to the central court, they were relatively independent of it. This organization was initially implemented out of military necessity but it soon became a mechanism for assimilating populations, exacting services and goods, and punishing those who did not comply with these demands (D. Newbury 1987:170). *Umuheto,* a form of clientage between less powerful and more powerful lineages, appears to have grown in importance at this time. Under this form of clientage less powerful cattle-owning lineages gave a cow or cows to more powerful lineages in return for protection of their herds (Des Forges 1972:5–6; Vansina 1962:65). Over time, the war chiefs seem to have started taking over the functions of the lineage heads, settling disputes and appropriating the right to distribute vacant lands, eroding the power of the lineage heads, and shrinking the effective functioning unit of the lineage (Des Forges 1972; Vansina 1962).

The process of erosion of lineage power seems to have been accelerated when the *baami* (kings) asserted their exclusive right to control land by enlarging the powers of the *abanyabutaka,* "men of the land." These men, who had been responsible for provisioning the Royal Court when it resided in a region, became responsible for collecting an annual tribute in kind from the agriculturalists. Agriculturalists, now called "Hutu," who received land from these chiefs, owed "labor service," *uburetwa,* in which they worked two out of every five days for the land chief. This new institution began to redirect the focus of power from the lineage to chiefs appointed from above (Des Forges 1972:7; Rwabukumba and Mudandagizi 1974:7, 10–11; Vansina 1962:68–70). This process intensified differentiation at the lineage level. Joseph Rwabukumba and Vincent Mudandagizi argue that the clientage relationships, like *umuheto* (lineage-based clientage), though based on lineages, linked the fortunes of different lineage segments to those of their particular patrons rather than to the fortunes of the larger lineage group (Rwabukumba and Mudandagizi 1974:18–19).

Over time, the land chiefs and the war chiefs claimed common lands that they appropriated and distributed to clients. The majority of these lands were common pasture lands. In response to this development, it appears that Yuhi Gahindiro established a new set of officials, *abanyamukenke* (men of the grass) to assert Court control over pasture land and to collect prestations for its use (Des Forges 1972:3). To break up the territories controlled by the powerful chiefs, he also created "small personal holdings" called *ibikingi* that he distributed to his favorites (Vansina 1962:70–71; Vidal 1969:396). These people controlled all rights over that land, could take on clients and exact tribute, and were not responsible to the local chiefs, only to the *mwami* (Rwabukumba and Mudandagizi 1974:13).

Associated with these changes was the development of a form of "personal clientage" called *ubuhake,* and of "land clientage," *isambu.* In the former, the relationship was marked by the transfer of the usufruct of a cow from the patron to the client. In the latter, a form of heritable tenure over land was given in return for payments in kind. Both of these relationships could be revoked at the whim of the patron. During this time *uburetwa,* "land clientage linked to labor service," continued to grow in importance. As these forms of clientage became more widespread, the *mwami* (king) used these institutions to his own advantage, asserting a hierarchy of clientage in which the king was the supreme patron. The effective lineage unit became progressively smaller, as members of the same lineages were drawn into different relationships based on clientage and locality (Des Forges 1972:7–8; Rwabukumba and Mudandagizi 1974:13–15; Vansina 1962:68–70; Vidal 1969:396).

LATE-NINETEENTH-CENTURY RWANDAN HISTORY (1865–1898)

KIGERI RWABUGIRI AND THE CENTRALIZATION OF POWER

It was *Mwami* Kigeri Rwabugiri (1865–1895) who thoroughly consolidated the system of clientage, smashed the power of the lineages, and centralized the powers of the chiefs.[4] Rwabugiri's expansion of his kingdom through conquest was accompanied by the wholesale extermination or incorporation of a previously independent lineage-based elite and the systematic appropriation of lineage, community, and fallow lands (Rwabukumba and Mudandagizi 1974:19). Alison Des Forges tells us that Rwabugiri "brought the notables to heel" through " ruthless terror and skillful manipulation of rivalries" (Des Forges 1972:13). He was able to replace the independent, hereditary chiefs with men who were dependent on him for their positions. To extend their control, these chiefs, in turn, instituted clientage relationships with the local population. The appropriation of land, the destruction of the lineage system, and growing population density made these ties increasingly necessary for peasant survival.

The expansion of the Rwandan kingdom was not a smooth and relentless conquest of the neighboring kingdoms and regions. Rather, it grew and contracted under different reigns until the mideighteenth century to the end of the nineteenth century when there was a systematic push into the peripheries. Tutsi colonialism, especially after the seventeenth century, appears to have followed a distinct pattern. It seems that the newly incorporated areas were first placed under the rule of different lineage-based war chiefs and armies.

Although these chiefs ruled the region, the king *(mwami)* also established a residence controlled by a wife or by a favorite. A process of assimilation took place through the armies and Tutsi settlers. Local cattle-holding lineages came to be considered Tutsi, while local agriculturalists were considered "non-Tutsi," and over time were classed as "Hutu." This history of warfare, conquest, and assimilation happened more often with kingdoms we would consider to be "Tutsi" than "Hutu." As the kingdom expanded groups were incorporated as Hutu[5] if they were predominantly farmers, or as Tutsi if they were predominantly herders, and aristocrats of both "groups" were assimilated and intermarried with the old aristocracy. Over time this kingdom became a highly effective colonial kingdom. It was also a kingdom in which the nature of power changed over time and these changes had political, social, economic, and cultural implications. As the power of the Tutsi elite grew in the region, the kingdom began to impose other aspects of central administration on these colonized regions, until they were fully incorporated into the central kingdom. As the administrative system was extended into the peripheries of the kingdom, the system of clientage and land tenure was spread even further downward affecting all levels of society. Where control was more recent, such as in the southwest and in the northwest, many forms of tenure and leadership coexisted. Despite the unprecedented power of this organization, at the time of German colonialism, the Tutsi kingdom only had tenuous control over much of the north and had only just integrated a good part of the east. Nevertheless, by the beginning of the twentieth century, the majority of the population in the consolidated regions was part of a dependent peasantry.

THE LINEAGE SYSTEM, LAND TENURE, KINSHIP, AND INHERITANCE

The two important units of the kinship system in Rwanda were the clan *(ubwoko)* and the lineage *(umuryango)*. The clan was not a corporate group; instead it provided a social identity for its members (C. Newbury 1988:96). The lineage, a patrilineal group that can "trace its agnatic ties to a common ancestor, usually 3 to 6 generations in the past, and who bear a common name" (C. Newbury 1988:95), formerly, held common rights over land and cattle (C. Newbury 1988:97). The head of the lineage[6] had the right to distribute unused lineage lands that were without direct heirs, and to accept clients and distribute land to them (Des Forges 1972:2; Gravel 1968a:118–121; Maquet 1961a:33–34; C. Newbury 1988:97; Rwabukumba and Mudandagizi 1974:11). Individual adult men controlled the distribution of land to their sons, and with population growth, increasing pressure on land, and new forms of land tenure, this distribution could create remarkable disparity between brothers and cousins even in one generation (Meschy 1974:40–41, 50–51). Women had rights to use common property lands allocated by their own lineage if they did not marry or if they divorced. The appropriation of the common lands and reduction of lineage lands, however, effectively ended women's access to land in Rwanda. Over time, both kinship and gender relations came to resemble clientage ties. Ethel M. Albert argues that in Rwanda and Burundi "the inferiority of women as women is only a special case of the general form of inferiority" (Albert 1971:188). The relationship of superior and inferior is a personal one and "everything depends on the will and affection of the superior . . . if he wishes, he will take back what he has already given in order to give it to someone he likes better. An inferior, whether serf . . . or wife . . . can only protest in vain" (Albert 1971:189–190).

COLONIAL RWANDA

The German Period (1898–1916)

In 1895 Kigeri Rwabugiri died and Mibambwe Rutarindwa, who had been ruling as coregnant for ten years, was enthroned. The queen-mother, Kanjogera, with her brothers, began a civil war to install her own son, Musinga, on the throne. During this civil war, control over the north was lost and control over the west became less secure. Musinga, a minor, was established on the throne in 1896. However, the independent reign of Musinga was short-lived. German colonial rule was established in 1898 when the Germans set up a military camp in Shangi, and the German colonial administration incorporated Rwanda into the "military region" of Ruanda—Urundi in 1899 (Des Forges 1972, 1986; C. Newbury 1988:122). In 1907, De Kandt was installed as Resident in Rwanda, creating an administrative post in Kigali (Nahimana 1987:116–118). However, Germany lost sovereignty during World War I. By 1916 the Belgians had penetrated Rwanda, and, although Belgian jurisdiction over Rwanda was not confirmed until the end of the war, de facto rule began at this time (Lemarchand 1970:63). The actual status of the state remained unclear until 1925, when Rwanda was declared a Belgian Protectorate by the League of Nations.

Throughout the whole German period, the German presence was very minimal. There were ten German nationals, soldiers, and administrators, in Rwanda at the beginning of World War I (Lemarchand 1970:63). From 1899 to 1907, the administration of Musinga was allowed to continue to rule Rwanda without active interference and he was able to expand his power into areas where the kingdom had only nominal control and to exact tribute and labor service (C. Newbury 1988:56–57, 121–122). Not only did this consolidate and expand the Rwandan kingdom, but, because of the way in which he was enthroned, it provided Musinga with a legitimacy he desperately needed.

Despite their minimal presence, the German administrators demanded large amounts of labor for transporting wood for building the new capital, Kigali, and for the construction of roads; the missions, which had been established at the turn of the century, also accelerated their labor demands. While both administrators and the mission paid their regular laborers salaries, they did not pay the unskilled laborers who were requisitioned through the notables. This arrangement enabled these notables and chiefs to increase the services and goods that they exacted for themselves (Des Forges 1972:318, 137). It became a common practice, for example, to demand three days *uburetwa* labor instead of two, out of a five-day week, and to force groups on the peripheries to do *uburetwa* (*corvée* labor) for the first time (Des Forges 1972:201).

BELGIAN COLONIAL RULE (1916–1961)

The initial occupation of the Belgians in 1916 saw an intensification of demands on labor and produce to meet wartime needs, as well as the division of the country into military districts (Des Forges 1969:187). Despite the policy of indirect rule, relations between the court and the Belgian administration were poor, especially in the period just after the war. The reasons for this were linked to the experiences of the Catholic Church in Rwanda, and the close link between the Belgian administration and the Peres Blancs. The Court was very hostile to the overtures of the Peres Blancs, who established the first churches in Rwanda, but, because the German administration had not been interested in promoting the cause of a French Catholic order, Musinga was able to use this division to weaken the demands of both the church and the administration. The Peres Blancs, excluded from the Court and unable to gain Tutsi converts, first recruited Hutu converts. They slipped easily into a patronage role vis-à-vis their converts, often using political influence to protect these converts from what they saw as unjust political and economic demands (Des Forges 1969:181).

Unlike the German administration, the Belgian administration was very sympathetic to the cause of the missions, and began to push for reforms for the Hutu peasantry. In 1917, the Resident was able to persuade Musinga to grudgingly institute land reforms, to reduce *uburetwa* labor service back to two days a week, and to protect peasants from arbitrary confiscations of their produce and wages. Most of these reforms worked to the advantage of the peasantry; however, the Belgians found the number of court cases dealing with clientage annoying and as part of these same "reforms" the Resident banned dissatisfied subjects or clients from seeking new patrons. This practice effectively destroyed the sole means for the Hutu to escape an oppressive lord (Des Forges 1972:218–219).

This Belgian interest in the peasantry and in political reform soon ended. Because they were not in a position to create their own bureaucracy, the Belgians grew increasingly committed to ruling through the king and the notables. The introduction of the Head Tax in 1917 emphasized the need for cooperation with the existing power structure because the chiefs and the notables had effectively undermined a similar tax instituted by the Germans (Des Forges 1972:234–235). The exactions that the Belgians demanded grew and with them the power and wealth of the chiefs and notables. The increasing Belgian commitment to indirect rule enabled the notables to exact harsher demands from the commoners, especially the Hutu, and "many Rwandans saw Belgian rule as the beginning of the 'time of the whip' " (Des Forges 1972:274).

"THE TIME OF THE WHIP"

In the 1920s, the administration introduced obligatory crop cultivation (as a famine relief measure), obligatory reforestation programs, and anti-erosion measures, and added systematic *corvée* labor *(akazi)* for road building and maintenance, drainage projects, and the construction of public buildings for the state to the "traditional" obligations already required by the lords. State projects were intensified in the 1930s, and a massive coffee-planting campaign was initiated (Chrétien 1978; Lemarchand 1977:78–79; C. Newbury 1988:112). The elite were encouraged to produce coffee, vegetables, and fruits for the market, using *corvée* labor (C. Newbury 1988:142). All of these activities were administered by the chiefs, who were responsible for mobilizing the required laborers for the *corvées*, collecting the taxes and enforcing the policies of the colonial regime. If the chiefs' demands were not met peasants were punished or evicted. To justify their actions, the chiefs simply maintained that the complainant refused to meet traditional obligations or Belgian exactions (Des Forges 1972:234–235).

These conditions of insecurity increasingly led peasants to enter into formal clientage relations (C. Newbury 1988:131–137). Clientage ties were not only a means to gain increased security of tenure, but also a means to escape the most degrading and menial tasks. The local chief decided who performed *corvée* labor, what kind, and how much. In theory, all adult men were obliged to perform *uburetwa* labor service; in reality "it was imposed specifically on the Hutu " (C. Newbury 1988:112). The Belgians publically deplored the behavior and the abuses of the chiefs, but for the most part ignored abuses. The pressures on the chiefs to meet European obligations were very intense. The monopoly of power enjoyed by the chiefs was contingent on meeting the demands of the Europeans. Failure to do so meant dismissal (C. Newbury 1988:142–145, 170).

Musinga and the Court fought every effort to alter the ruling elite's power and to allow the conversion of the Tutsi elite, so the Belgians set about educating a cadre of local administrators. Using the policy of divide and rule, they were able to reduce the authority of the most powerful chiefs by giving important roles to members of rival factions. In the end, they succeeded in dividing the Tutsi lords into two factions: the "modern" faction, which was prepared to collaborate and to work with the new colonial masters, and the "traditional" faction, which was headed by the *mwami* (king) and resisted the actions of the colonizers (Des Forges 1969; Lemarchand 1970:73–75; Vidal 1973:36). As Musinga's hostility to this "modern" group grew, the Belgians sought to dismantle the aspects of the indigenous administration system that fragmented the power of the chiefs and ensured royal control. In 1926, the Belgians began reforming the administrative structure into a vastly reduced hierarchy of chiefs and subchiefs. By 1931, the number of chiefs was reduced from several thousand to eleven hundred (Des Forges 1969:190). Half of these were either Belgian protégés or had some Western education. The net effect of these reforms was the emergence of a "far more starkly authoritarian system" (Lemarchand 1977:78). At the same time, the administration and the church began planning to remove Musinga. From 1929 on, they built a case against Musinga based on his active opposition to the church, "mismanagement" of the affairs of state, and "incompetence," and most bizarrely, recourse to sorcery. Restructuring of the administrative hierarchy enabled the Belgians to isolate him from his most "traditional" supporters. In 1931 the Europeans, with the active participation of the church, deposed him and replaced him with his son, Rudahigwa (Des Forges 1969:193–194).

Along with these reforms came a policy of establishing Tutsi supremacy by reserving educational opportunities for Tutsi and for excluding Hutu, and by replacing Hutu chiefs by pro-European Tutsi chiefs in the north (Des Forges 1969:190–191; Lemarchand 1977:77, 1970:72–73; C. Newbury 1988:112, 133, 281). The Belgians gave the missions full control over schooling in 1925, and most of the new schools enrolled the sons of the chiefs. The schools that were designated for training future administrators were deliberately restricted to Tutsi students alone (Des Forges 1969:198; Lemarchand 1970:73; Vidal 1973:35). There was also a change in attitude on the part of the administration and the church such that "[f]rom 1929 on, the Belgians began praising Tutsi intelligence and capacity for assimilation, a sharp contrast to their earlier condemnations of the retrograde spirit of the elite" (Des Forges 1969:191). The ideology of the period promoted the idea that the Tutsi were born to rule, and the policies of the administration and the church created an occupational caste, enabling the Belgians to replace chiefs who opposed them with "modern" chiefs (Chrétien 1985; Des Forges 1969:187). The Tutsi ruling elite played a role in this process. King Rudahigwa crystallized the "Tutsi ideology" through research and publications on his dynastic history (especially by the Abbé Kagame), through sports, arts, clothing, and through the choice of court members and members of foreign delegations (Chrétien 1985:146–147). "Traditional" Rwanda was essentially reconstructed during this period (Chrétien 1985:146). Research during the colonial period by both Tutsi and Europeans promoted "the vision . . . of a timeless feudal state" (Chrétien 1985:147, my translation). One of the most blatant cases of this bias is the study by Jacques J. Maquet who in his ethnography, *The Premise of Inequality*, states that he did not interview any Hutu because "the more competent people on political organization were the Tutsi," arguing that his "aim was not to assess the opinions and knowledge of the whole of the Ruanda population on their past political organization, but to discover *as accurately as possible* what that organization was" (Maquet 1961a:3, my emphasis). Needless to say he concluded that the system in Rwanda was beneficial to all concerned and that all accepted "the premise of inequality" as natural. This book was published during the height of anti-Tutsi violence at the time of independence.

The years that followed the installation of Rudahigwa saw the escalation of demands on the population through the chiefs and major changes in the system of *prestations*. To encourage wage labor, most were transformed into money payments in 1934. However, *uburetwa* remained unchanged because the administrators argued that it was a symbol of Hutu submission to authority (C. Newbury 1988:141–142). With the intensification of demands and *corvées*, there was an increase in out-migration. The 1920s and 1930s saw a mass movement of men to Uganda and to the Belgian Congo and into the wage labor market. In 1939, to encourage wage labor, the Belgians allowed *uburetwa* to be paid in cash by contract laborers and waived public works obligations. However these exemptions were often abused because the demands on chiefs were not relaxed. The wives of migrants and contract workers were forced to fulfill *uburetwa* as well as to meet government labor *corvées* and obligatory cultivation requirements. The chiefs, required to mobilize a fixed number of laborers each day, compelled the men who remained, to work far in excess of the legislated days (Chrétien 1978:92–94; C. Newbury 1988:142–143, 170). Using mission records, Jean-Pierre Chrétien calculated that in one high out-migration area, as many as half the available adult male population engaged in *corvée* labor each day (Chrétien 1978:93). In addition, the Belgians began a policy of encouraging the chiefs to undertake large-scale cash cropping, especially coffee and vegetables, with the use of *uburetwa* labor. At the same time, there was an expansion of public works projects and the intensification of obligatory crop cultivation. Moreover, European enterprises, such as plantations, industries, and mines, also demanded that the government provide labor. This was often done by ordering the chiefs to produce a set number of workers for a given day, and to pursue laborers who fled their contracts. Chiefs, who were not able to produce the required number, lost their positions. Although abuse of this system was necessary to meet the demands of the Europeans, it also permitted chiefs to accumulate considerable wealth and so strengthened chiefly power (Chrétien 1978; C. Newbury 1988:165–176).

The introduction of "native tribunals" in 1936 only increased the power of the Tutsi lords because these were headed only by Tutsi chiefs. They were used to expand Tutsi power and to legitimize abuses (Lemarchand 1970:75–76). It is not surprising that Belgian reform after the Second World War did nothing to improve the situation of the peasantry. In 1949, *uburetwa* labor service was replaced by a monetary tax and in 1954 *ubuhake* (cattle clientage) was abolished; however, little changed. Land clientage was not abolished and pasture land remained in the hands of the chiefs. *Uburetwa* labor service still continued in many regions, and peasants with cattle, were still required to render services to lords in return for access to pastures and agricultural land (C. Newbury 1988:146). At the close of the colonial period, the Tutsi elite held considerable power. Reforms were largely ineffective, or actually favored the growth of power of this political and economic elite.

However, the Belgian colonial policies were changing, through pressure from the United Nations and from the new Belgian clergy and administrators who were of "relatively humble social origins" and so "were more generally disposed to identify with the plight of the Hutu masses" (Lemarchand 1970:134, 138). By the late 1940s and 1950s, the Belgians faced strong pressure from the UN to reform the administrative system. However, the reforms had little effect, leaving the peasants "faced with virtually all the inconveniences of the clientage relationship while being deprived of the advantages it once offered" (Lemarchand 1977:82). New forms of control over "labor, land, educational opportunities, wealth, and, most important, access to the state apparatus" had consolidated power in the hands of a few (C. Newbury 1988:147). The revolutionary political events of the 1950s and 1960s grew out of this situation.

Clientage, Land Tenure, Common Property, and Labor Relations during the Colonial Period

In the precolonial period, the centralization of power and the expansion of the state crushed the lineages, placing control over land, labor, and cattle in the hands of the elite in the central region of Rwanda. On the peripheries, which had been more recently assimilated, this process seriously undermined the power of the lineages but had not yet completely replaced it. The policies of the colonial period extended the central kingdom's control into all the regions. The clientage relationships that were still based on lineage ties, such as *umuheto*, were abolished in the reforms of the 1920s, and ties between individuals were accentuated. *Uburetwa* was made universal, and European taxes and levies "were imposed on individual adult men and not lineages" (C. Newbury 1988:112). The instabilities arising out of the growing power of the chiefs drove more peasants to seek *ubuhake* labor clientage and land clientage, but this process also augmented the coercive power of the lords. More and more control over land and labor passed into the hands of the elite and clientage became more exploitative (Des Forges 1972:349; Lemarchand 1970:73–75; C. Newbury 1988:17–18, 98–112, 1978:24–25; Vidal 1973:39).

Postcolonial Rwanda (1961–1994)

The anti-Tutsi rhetoric grew in intensity in the 1950s and the new Belgian administration and the missions championed the new "natural" rulers of Rwanda, the Hutu. The years 1959 to 1961 saw considerable turbulence and bloodshed. Initially anti-Tutsi sentiments took the form of land invasions and the harassment of Tutsi who were powerful, affluent, or well connected; however this soon escalated into bloodshed (Codere 1973). The death of the old king, the enthronement of Ndahindurwa, and the elections in 1959 precipitated the overthrow of the Tutsi and the institution of a Hutu-led government. Bloody ethnic fighting broke out after the elections and the *mwami* (king), who had been installed by an extremist elite faction, mobilized his troops to uphold the power of the most repressive of the lords. This action only exacerbated the situation. In 1961, the *mwami* was deposed, anti-Tutsi reprisals continued, and the UN intervened. In the 1961 elections the Hutu parties won a sweeping majority and a referendum abolished the monarchy. In 1962, the Parmehutu Party was elected to power with Gregoire Kayibanda as president. The first and only elected Rwandan government drew its strength from a pro-Hutu, racist ideology that claimed the Hutu held the racial right to rule Rwanda (C. Newbury 1980, 1988). In keeping with its peers in other parts of Africa, the "First Republic," as this regime is known, declared a one-party state and ended multiparty democracy in Rwanda.

This government became increasingly corrupt. By the late 1960s and early 1970s it had concentrated access to resources, opportunities, and power into the hands of a tiny elite based in central and southern Rwanda. In 1973, faced with opposition from northern factions, who began to be openly critical of the regime, and the growing discontent of the poor, who began to attack the rich, Kayibanda attempted to incite ethnic violence in the schools and in the university. However, Kayibanda lost control of this process and the Parmehutu Party fell to a northern coup d'état on July 5, 1973 (C. Newbury 1992:197–198; Reyntjens 1994:29). This was a very popular coup, because it reduced ethnic violence and the level of government corruption in Rwanda (Reyntjens 1994:29). Filip Reyntjens argues that "it is forgotten that President Habyarimana was particularly popular with Tutsi in the country, and that he was accused of favoring this group by some Hutu groups" (Reyntjens 1994:35–36, my translation). The anti-Tutsi rhetoric of the regime ebbed and flowed. There is no question that the elected government of Kayibanda made sporadic use of "Tutsi-bashing." During the beginning of the second regime, known as the "Second Republic," Hutu-Tutsi relations were often quite amicable and, although positions at the top were confined to Hutu (predominantly drawn from the north), there was some mobility for Tutsi especially in the south. There was also considerable intermarriage, not only between southern Tutsi and Hutu, but also between northern Hutu families and economically powerful Tutsi families.[7]

By 1989, Habyarimana was facing a crisis similar to Kayibanda's in 1973. There was growing discontent with his regime and at the same time the country was required to undergo major economic restructuring. The invasion by the Rwandan Patriotic Front, the majority of whom were Tutsi, provided a propaganda opportunity that deflected criticism of the military regime. The origins of this crisis and these struggles were rooted in the policies and crises of the late 1980s and 1990s. The interclass conflicts arose out of the policies of the Habyarimana regime in the late 1980s and early 1990s, during which the disparity between rich and poor grew enormously throughout the country and the political and social distance between elites and the predominantly rural poor grew as well (C. Newbury 1992:203; Reyntjens 1994:32, fns. 47, 33).

POLITICAL, ECONOMIC, AND SOCIAL STRUCTURE UNDER THE TWO REPUBLICS (1961–1994)

The legacy of the precolonial and colonial states could be seen in the structures of the new regimes. Patron-client ties shifted from Tutsi-Hutu to ties within the "Hutu stratum" (Lemarchand 1977:89). The development of a Hutu identity and politics on the part of a Hutu middle class "expanded" the practice of political clientalism to encompass the whole state (Chrétien 1985:156). Access to government jobs, education, land, and government-controlled resources still depended on informal clientage ties (Lemarchand 1982:4, 14, 31). Like the clientage ties of the previous eras, these ties were based on individual relations and were situated in the context of a very strong sense of hierarchy. The legacy of Rwandan history could also be seen in other forms. Government *corvée* labor still existed, disguised as *umuganda* (cooperative labor service), which was extended to encompass all adult men and women. Just like the chiefs before them, the appointees who delegated this work doled out the best jobs as rewards to their clients and the poorest jobs as punishments. The practice of appropriating unpaid labor for influential outsiders, such as development projects, was still routinely practiced. Obligatory cultivation, as a famine relief measure, still continued and was still actively disliked. Policies that enforced coffee cultivation were still in place. Ethnicity still conditioned access to resources such as high-level government jobs, education, and land. However, for most peasants, both Hutu and Tutsi, the privileges accorded by ethnicity were meaningless. It was still a minority within the elite group that profited from ethnic affiliations.

Nevertheless, the political ideology on which both republics were founded provided some mobility for the peasantry and enabled some to gain access to certain forms of resources, depending on the region of Rwanda. Because the state was founded on the idea that it represented "the majority" and was dismantling an externally imposed feudalism, the land and resources of the Tutsi elites was redistributed in the areas where they were the most powerful, the south and center regions of Rwanda; consequently land was redistributed in these regions at the beginning of the 1960s. In the north, "when the [Habyarimana] government took power, their ambition was to restore their own pre-Tutsi culture: a culture dominated by powerful landlords *(abakonde)* who attracted clients *(abagererwa)* through the release of land" (Pottier 1990:4). This ideology led to a large disparity in the size and types of land holdings between rich and poor in different regions in Rwanda. However, the ideology of being a broad-based government and the institution of the "Developmental State" under Habyarimana created a larger pool of clients. In theory, all of the Hutu peasantry were clients of the state and often less valuable resources could be made available to the peasantry. This factor strongly affected the nature of land tenure and common property resource use in Rwanda. This affected both the nature of the industries under study and the economic changes that created the crisis that helped precipitate genocide.

LAND TENURE AND COMMON PROPERTY SYSTEMS UNDER THE TWO REPUBLICS (1961–1994)

At the time of independence most land in Rwanda was in the hands of the elite. It was farmed by peasants on the basis of one-to-one relations established with the elite. However, there were still small plots of lands held by individuals. These were either lineage lands that had been continuously occupied and had never been seized by the state or lands acquired through other means, for instance, through direct sale or as gifts from a patron. All these lands, whether controlled by the elite or held by individuals, were in the hands of men. Postindependence land tenure was a complex combination of various degrees of "private" ownership, customary rights, and government ownership. Some of the land that had been in the hands of the elite was redistributed, particularly in the south; some was directly appropriated by the state and/or subjected to various degrees of state control. Access to some kinds of land was controlled by powerful men, who redistributed this land on a variety of bases that ranged from the receipt of cash payment to the securing of special favors, enabling them to gain access to labor (Lemarchand 1982:32). The Rwandan state retained the ultimate ownership of all land and the state placed severe restrictions on land sales. The postindependence government reinstituted lineage rights over some cultivated land, gave some tenants rights to cultivated lands received through clientage, and placed control of other lands into the hands of the *communes* (Meschy 1973:72). Although for the majority of the population the rights over the use of land became much more stable after independence in 1961, nevertheless, both the First and Second republics saw the concentration of lands in the hands of the government elite and their clients.

There were two forms of privately held lands, neither of which could be sold without government permission: lineage lands and lands acquired through nonlineage sources.[8] Lineage lands were partly regulated by "customary rights" and controlled by the lineage head, an inherited position. The lineages had no surplus or communal lands at their disposal. All lineage lands were now held by individuals. The lineage did not redistribute land that was occupied, nor did the lineage head exercise any control over inheritance or land use (Fairhead 1990:59–63, 179–185). The main function of the lineage was control over the sale of lineage land held by individuals or the distribution of land with no direct heirs (Meschy 1973:73–74). This form of land tenure involved a "renegotiation of tradition" because the reinterpretation of the lineage system in modern law still excluded women, who had previously had rights over land. Land acquired through other sources,[9] that is, given to a man by a political authority or purchased, was controlled by the lineage segment directly descended from the recipient and was not regulated by the rules applied to lineage lands. These lands could be owned by men or women[9] and could be sold without consent of the lineage.

Vacant lands, deserted lands, and valley bottomlands were directly controlled by the *communes*, which had the right to distribute up to 2 hectares per person.[10] Unexploited communal lands could be used as pasture by all inhabitants of the *commune*. Lands given by the *commune* could be sold only after the family receiving them had worked the land in some way (Meschy 1974:43). There was a distinction made between land on the lower slopes of the hills, forested land,[12] and marsh and valley bottomland (Meschy 1973:72).[11] However, none of this land was ever distributed systematically; rather, patronage played an important role in gaining and retaining control over public lands.

Wooded lands were regulated by a special system. The land was communal but management of trees varied. In some cases, trees were individually owned and every member of the *secteur* had the right to plant trees on land set aside for that purpose (Meschy 1973:78). In others, trees were owned by the *commune*, which then controlled the conditions under which they were harvested. Despite the fact that woodland was communally owned, few of the small peasant producers in my survey had access to this type of land, although most could gather branches for cooking fuel from these areas. The large amount of wood required to fire the kilns was most often bought from a mix of sources. The large producers in my study were often able to gain access to trees from these woodlands, which provided them with a steady source of cheap wood, through established ties with local officials

Tenure of marshland and valley bottomland was a somewhat different case and, as the main site of clay land, is of special significance to this study. Prior to the revolution it was reserved for dry season pasture for Tutsi-owned herds. Just after independence many families acquired access through land invasions, which quickly came to be regulated through the *communes*. Soon after, access to these lands was based on patronage. "Ownership" had to be confirmed through the *commune*, so that even land gained through de facto occupation had to be retained through cash payments or through other services, and officials could transfer it as they deemed fit. Fields had to be worked, by either the owner or a tenant, or they could be lost (Meschy 1974:50, 77). Most often the plots held by families in the marshes were used to provide the majority of dry season crops. Marshland was often taken back by the *commune* and used for projects, given to cooperatives and other groups, or taken over by functionaries for their own use. Tenure over marsh and valley bottomland was always very uncertain. Since use of all resources in the valley bottoms was controlled by the *commune*, it strongly influenced the patterns of clay excavation in many of these areas. A few powerful men played a major role in determining the scale of the enterprises found in any location.

LAND, LABOR, AND POWER IN RWANDA

Although the early history of Rwanda is a matter of debate and speculation, the coexistence of multiple tenure systems and the regional diversity indicate a history of conquest and assimilation. When the Germans established their colonial power in 1898, the majority of the peasantry in central Rwanda was impoverished. To gain access to land, men were required to enter into various direct personal relations with patrons. For the peasantry, clientage was often the best option. Even so these relations did not guarantee survival and peasants were frequently reduced to selling their labor to make ends meet and to fulfill their obligations. In certain regions of central Rwanda, Claudine Vidal argues, as much as 50 percent of the peasantry was forced to sell their labor on a regular basis. She maintains that this figure represents only those who worked for others and who never hired labor. By the end of the nineteenth century, Vidal insists that virtually all peasants in central and parts of southern Rwanda were forced to sell labor at some time or another. Among the poorest peasants, both men and women sold their labor, but more commonly the man would sell his labor and the woman would work her husband's land (Vidal 1974:58–64). In the recently assimilated peripheries, such as the Cyangugu area and the north, where the central administration had a less powerful hold, wage labor appears to have been considerably less common. Clientage ties, however, grew increasingly important, as pasture lands, fallow lands, and other common lands were appropriated by the state. Where lineage lands still existed, increasing pressure on land forced young men into clientage relations to gain access to adequate land, undermining the power of the lineage heads and transforming power relations within the household (C. Newbury 1988). The elite, who by 1898 were mostly Tutsi, saw themselves as distinctly superior to both poor Hutu and poor Tutsi.[12] Still, it is critical to remember that the vast majority of the Tutsi were commoners who had more in common with the Hutu peasants than with the Tutsi lords, while the Hutu lords, who formed a minority in the elite, had little in common with the Hutu peasants who they exploited (Chrétien 1985:150; C. Newbury 1978:21, 1988:13; Vidal 1969:399).

The German and Belgian colonial administrations, through their policies of indirect rule and their racist theories, consolidated the power of a fraction of the Tutsi elite and transformed ethnicity into a vastly simplified racial category. The "reforms" instituted by these administrations, the increased demands on labor, and the simplification of the ruling structure of the Court, which purged the Hutu elite out of political power and tied power to the capacity to meet European demands, intensified the exploitation of the peasantry and centralized land, labor, and power into the hands of a tiny elite, legitimized by a racist ideology and buttressed by exclusionary policies that posited a "superior race," the Tutsi, ruling by natural superiority over the "inferior race," the Hutu. Most of the peasantry were heavily taxed and tied into clientage relations that allowed them access to land that made heavy demands on their labor and incomes. The legislation that banned these relations did nothing to change the structures under which the majority of commoners, Tutsi and Hutu, lived.

The violent events of 1959 to 1961 led to the overthrow of the aristocracy and to the installation of an elected government, which soon declared itself a one-party state. Although initial reforms appeared to broaden the base of access to resources and power in Rwanda, both the First Republic and the Second centralized land, labor, and power into the hands of a new elite. Under the

First Republic, the beneficiaries were Hutu elites drawn from the south and center of Rwanda. Under the Second Republic, the beneficiaries were from the northwest. The ideology underpinning both of these regimes led to considerable regional differences. The lands of the dispossessed Tutsi elite were redistributed in the south, while the reestablishment of "traditional" structures in the northwest led to larger disparity in access to land and resources. Access to the benefits of the state continued to be tied to clientage relations; however these were somewhat modified by the need to maintain a semblance of providing a broad-based government that represented the "majority." The major benefits of the state, higher education, government positions, and access to the most lucrative resources continued to be controlled by a tiny elite for its own benefit; however, less lucrative resources were often extended to the population. Under the two republics, access to primary education, medical care, and clean water expanded for the majority of the peasantry, although these benefits differed by region depending on the clique in power.

The history of centralization of land, resources, and power; the development of regional diversity; the transformation of the lineage system; gender relations; the recasting of ethnicity in precolonial and colonial Rwanda; and the reconfiguration of these structures in the postcolonial state have profoundly influenced the development of the brick- and tile-making industries in Rwanda as well as the organization of labor. These changes also had a profound impact on the postcolonial politics of Rwanda and on the microlevel domestic/household politics of Rwanda. At the state level, the nature of Tutsi rule in Rwanda enabled the regime of Habyarimana to demonize the Tutsi after the Rwandan Patriotic Front invasion and fueled the propaganda campaign. The nature of land tenure, clientage, and growing corruption made it necessary for an increasingly beleaguered government to resort to this form of propaganda to prop up a government that was losing credibility, as I will show in chapter 7. At the household level, as I will show in chapters 5 to 7, these transformations influenced the capacity of the head of the household to control his or her family's labor, the capacity of the wife to control the product of her labor and the nature of inheritance, and a woman's capacity to enter into entrepreneurial activity.

5

"Your Patron Begets You"

Household Reproduction, Gender and Domestic Relations, and Access to Family Labor

Habyara shôbuja ntíhabyará só: Your patron and not your father is the one who begets you says the Rwanda proverb used to justify the loss of children's aid to a more powerful man (Crepeau and Bizimana 1979:131). The transformation of paternal control over resources and the impact of precolonial and colonial social relations, has produced a situation in which a household head cannot easily control the labor of grown children. In my study, family members did not see themselves as undertaking a collective family project. Moreover, women rarely owned critical resources but were responsible for household subsistence, while men had the right to control almost all surplus produced by women with little obligation to contribute to household subsistence. In almost every case, the small peasant producers and pieceworkers in the study did not earn the larger part of their livelihood through these industries. Most of the men lived in households that could be considered largely "self-provisioning," that is to say that most of the foodstuffs consumed by the household were produced by their wives.[1] This chapter examines the impact of the precolonial transformations in land and labor on the availability of household labor, and considers the role of self-provisioning and its effect on the reproduction[2] of small industries, wage labor, and the household in Rwanda.

PATTERNS OF LAND INHERITANCE

The precolonial and colonial transformations in land and labor affected household relations and the growth of differentiation within lineage segments and even between brothers and half-brothers. Ideally all sons should inherit some land. As in the pre-independence period, individual men almost always controlled inheritance, which took place at the time of marriage.[3] The father decided how the land was to be divided and the quantity, quality, and location of the land that was inherited by each son was completely within his control (Meschy 1973:72–74). Unequal and capricious inheritance was often the source of considerable ill feeling and acrimonious disputes between brothers (Fairhead 1990:58–59, 182–184; Meschy 1973:74), as in the following example drawn from my field notes:

> My father's brothers did not want to recognize his right to inherit because he was born to a woman who quickly divorced her husband, my grandfather. My father had to move and only returned under the force of justice *(sous la force du justice)*. At [the other location], we had only a tiny bit of land. The other half brothers wanted all our father's land for themselves.

Siblings are considered to be adversaries as the Rwandan proverb *Urwâgano rw nône rwbanje m nda imwé:* The hatred of today began in the womb (Crepeau and Bizimana 1979:553) illustrates.

The realities of unequal inheritance, land pressure, and family size meant that there was considerable inequality between members of the same family. The final outcome of this system of inheritance was the fragmentation of landholdings and the development of a lineage land system in which individual holdings varied greatly between families in the same lineage and between families of different lineages (Meschy 1973:78–79). This inequality was exacerbated by the fact that parents often favored certain sons and encouraged the 'buying-off' of the rights of the other sons (Meschy 1974:51). The common pattern for these landless, or virtually landless, sons has been migration to Uganda or to the Democratic Republic of Congo (Chrétien 1978:71–102; Meschy 1973:79; C. Newbury 1988:152–179). I have collected quite a number of cases of this kind of migration, especially in the north, where land distribution is quite unequal. One case was particularly striking. The young man told me that

> I don't have any land because I left for Uganda and, when I came back, my parents had sold everything and left for Zaïre. They had a lot of debts and to pay them back they were obliged to sell their land. Once they were landless they left for Zaïre and most of the family preferred to join them. At this time I was in Uganda. I don't know how things have worked out in Zaïre for them. I'm living on the parcel of land that used to be my parents' but I have no land. Renting land is difficult, the owners are often mean. If you produce a great deal [on their land] they can take back the land.

His landlord was his uncle. In theory, all lineage members are entitled to a share of land, but without the clout to enforce this rule, peasants are often not able to reclaim any land.

LAND INHERITANCE AND CLIENTALISM

This pattern of inheritance, favoritism, and the limits of paternal power has to be considered in the light of the development of clientalism and the increasing pressure on land. The power of the father to control his sons lasted only until the time of inheritance, and a son could demand his inheritance a few years before he planned to marry (Fairhead 1990:182–184). Jim Freedman argues that a central aspect of control of elders over juniors in the traditional lineage system was the capacity to control access to the surplus necessary for juniors to marry. This control diminished, especially in the north, with encroachment by the central state and increasing demographic pressure (Freedman 1984:86–90). In the north and the south, clientage was a major avenue of access to lands, wealth, and power. At best the father could be considered only one form of patron, one who controlled access to a rapidly dwindling resource. This had a profound impact on the nature and organization of the smaller brick and tile industries in Rwanda.

LAND INHERITANCE, ACCESS TO FAMILY LABOR, AND BRICK AND ROOF TILE PRODUCTION

Inheritance, marriage, and the developmental cycle of the family all played a role in the capacity of men to establish and continue a business. Inheritance was an important factor because it gave men access to agricultural lands. Since the tile industries are a seasonal enterprise, these men could produce cash crops in the rainy seasons. The income they earned in these seasons, if they had sufficient lands, could be used to start an enterprise. The following example illustrates the role of both inheritance and marriage in the evolution of these enterprises.

Chrysanthe, an affluent young man, used his inheritance to enter directly into tile production in 1979 using hired labor, while his younger brother, Laurent, was able to enter into a small-scale tile enterprise only by working with others or alone. These two young men, neither of whom had a history of wage work before beginning tile production, began with different resources as the result of unequal inheritance. This differentiation between brothers was not rare. They often began with very uneven resources, as the case of Theodomir and his brothers illustrated in chapter 3.

Marriage played an even more important role in the capacities of most of the small peasant producers to enter into business or to expand their enterprises. Most men who were able to build a kiln or to begin hiring labor, did so after marriage. In Gatovu, of the 16 men who worked in this way, 13 were married; of the 20 in Gatovu who worked with others or alone, 9 were married; and of 13 of the men in Ngoma who worked on the latter model, 7 were married. Only 3 men in Gatovu were able to establish an enterprise that ran on the basis of hired labor. These men started with enough capital to enter into brick production at this level.

Most of the men, in both locations, began their enterprises around the time of their marriage or at the time they inherited land and began to build a home. Like Gakuzi in chapter 4, some were able to use the income generated from other jobs to start up. Others used the cash they generated by selling cash crops produced during the rainy season. Like Juvenal, a number of men started their enterprises before they married, then expanded their operations at the time of marriage. Women's agricultural labor and women's responsibility for household reproduction allowed men to invest the surplus generated by cash crops and/or by their small enterprises outside of the household. This investment enabled them the flexibility to weather changes in the market and provided the capital to invest in their enterprises. Men like Gakuzi were often able to start a business only when they had access to this kind of female labor.

This reliance on female labor notwithstanding, none of these small peasant producers used other forms of family labor within their industries. The nature of precolonial and colonial social relations, coupled with the expansion of the wage sector after independence, created a situation where men have very little control over the labor of grown sons in the south. This lack of control was reflected in the production strategies used by most men and affected the development of the petty commodity enterprises. Inheritance and marriage allowed men to establish and then to expand an enterprise, but this could only be accomplished on the basis of group work or hired labor. None of the small peasant producers expanded their enterprises again when their children were old enough to enter production. The two informants who had retired had worked on this basis for more than fifteen years and then retired in their early sixties because they found the work had become too hard. Neither of their sons took over their business. Except for one case, there was a complete absence of household labor within these enterprises.

Most of the men in my survey worked alone or pooled their resources with others; virtually none worked with kin or household labor. A glance at the economies of scale (table 1 in chapter 2) shows that access to cheap labor or labor available through noneconomic means was critical to these enterprises. In the Mexican brickyards, Scott Cook claims that "the viability of the capitalist brickyard enterprise resides in its ability to engage several laborers for the price of one," arguing that the use of family labor power "is not so much 'self-exploitation' as it is the systematic use of the labor power of others in the worker-proprietor's household . . ." (Cook 1984:187). He assumes that this category of labor is always available.

THE HOUSEHOLD, SMALL PEASANT PRODUCTION, AND DOMESTIC RELATIONS

Recently, there has been growing recognition that the household is not a "unitary social actor." Rather, to understand household dynamics intra- and interhousehold relations must be examined and analyzed (Guyer and Peters 1987:205, 207; Hart 1992; Jackson 1993; Whitehead 1984; Yanagisako 1979:175). Earlier critiques pointed out that ideas about relations within the household are often based on preconceptions about kin relations that "are imbued in most cultures with ideas of natural behavior, [and] natural morality" (Harris 1981:139, 144), along with such concepts as pooling, sharing, and generosity. This understanding has led to a new discussion of power, authority, and gender relations within the household (Carney and Watts 1990); which, in turn, has begun to call into question our assumptions about relations between generations. It is critical to ask how producers maintain control over, and secure the availability of, household and family labor, recognizing that members of a household "possess not just different but opposed economic interests" (Brass 1986:59). Because an individual might "derive more benefit from selling his or her own labor-power on the open market," it becomes necessary "to identify the countervailing mechanisms which prevent this from happening" (Brass 1986:59–60). In Rwanda, the countervailing mechanisms are not strong.

The Rwandan Household

In 1983, most households in central Rwanda were composed of the conjugal pair and their children living in a "compound," *rugo*. The compounds were dotted over the countryside in a dispersed settlement pattern. Married children established themselves in their own compounds. The son built a house on lands he inherited when he was old enough to marry. Women moved to the compounds of their husbands. Polygynous marriages, while illegal, were socially acceptable. Each wife and her children had their own compound, and the wife farmed the fields set aside for her by her husband. Divorce was quite common. If the couple divorced, the woman returned to her own family and the husband kept his land and, if the bride-price had been paid, the children as well.

In a survey of 214 households in Gatovu, only 26 included residents who were not members of the nuclear family. Of these, 10 were domestic and agricultural laborers, often related by distant kin ties, or orphans between the ages of 10 and 15, most likely also domestic or agricultural laborers. Eleven households had children of children living with them. Most often these were children of divorced or deceased sons, or of unmarried daughters. Two households were sheltering women who had fled their husbands.[4] Three households had aged mothers living with them. More commonly an aged mother lived in an adjacent *rugo*, but was supported by her son and his children.

The sons of each wife were given their inheritance from among the fields that their mother worked.[5] While young children worked with their mother on the land, it was uncommon to see older male children working with the mother (Habimana 1973:753). The husband might work with his wife during peak periods if he had only one wife. However, it was uncommon for a man in a polygynous marriage to work with any of his wives (Voss, personal communication). There were relatively few interhousehold links, and children felt no obligation to work with parents. Most of the income generated by either the wife or the husband was controlled by the husband, but neither controlled the income of their children. For example, none of the children working in the brickyards as porters in Huye was expected to contribute their income to their families. Over the course of my research it became clear that in Rwanda it was the conjugal pair, and not the household, which was the economic unit, and that the income and production of this unit was under the control of the husband.

This situation arose out of the transformation of land tenure and lineage structures in the precolonial and colonial states. By the turn of the century, in central Rwanda lineages had virtually no function. The household head of a poor household had little more at his disposal than his own labor power and that of his wife and young children. Most were compelled to sell their labor to survive. Affluent households were those that could hire labor (Codere 1973:246–247; Vidal 1974:68). Each of these productive units worked its own patrimony and lived in its own compound, built apart from the others. Such a unit could only count on its own labor or, if sufficiently wealthy, the labor it was able to hire or otherwise extract from others. There were strategies for gaining access to labor, but these required a substantial surplus, which most peasant households were unable to generate (Vidal 1974:60). Households in precolonial Rwanda were not completely self-sufficient. A market economy already existed by the nineteenth century (Lugan 1977, 1981; Lugan and Nyagahene 1983; C. Newbury 1988; D. Newbury 1980b). This market was nonmonetary, but each item could be transacted for any other,[6] and it dealt equally in subsistence goods and luxury goods (Lugan 1981; Lugan and Nyahagene 1983). Even a household whose harvest was sufficient for its own subsistence, and for its prestations and obligations, still had to work outside the holding to gain access to other goods. Those few who had sufficient surplus were able to obtain the labor power necessary to create further surplus (Vidal 1974:68).

As already noted, the mobility of labor, the commodified nature of labor, the insecurity of inheritance, and the existence of a clientage system created a climate in which the labor of grown sons was not easily controlled. This situation was exacerbated by the fact that, given the polygynous nature of Rwandan society, men often invested in additional wives for themselves rather than for their sons. Some sons, in the central regions of Rwanda, needed to enter into a patron-client relationship that provided a cow or hoes in order to marry. During the colonial and postcolonial periods sons looked for wage-earning opportunities. These were gained most often through patronage. One would think that men would wield considerable power over sons by controlling land. However, in general, it was the mother's support of a particular son that gained him a larger portion of the inheritance (Albert 1971:209). The advent of colonialism and the penetration of capitalism in this milieu only intensified individualism. The opportunities open to sons increased while a man's capacity to control the labor of his son's decreased. Put in the terminology of Tom Brass, the "countervailing mechanisms" by which men retained the labor of their children no longer were very powerful.

KINSHIP, DOMESTIC RELATIONS, AND ACCESS TO LABOR

This weakness of the countervailing mechanisms of kinship had serious implications for the nature of domestic politics and for the organization of brick and tile industries in Rwanda. Even in the smallest industries, if men needed additional labor they were required to hire labor and did not use family labor. Only two out of sixty-nine entrepreneurs in my survey used any form of family labor: one had hired a brother and a half brother; the other had worked for his father but had started his own business after one season. Moreover, the incidence of polygyny and the low education level of the children of many long-established brick and tile makers clearly showed their disinterest in investing in their children. Instead, they invested in more wives. Men could not control the actions of their sons. The following was a typical response to a question about working with family members: "I had problems with my family all the time, so I started working on my own. I wanted to make my own decisions." The few men who had worked with a father characteristically left when they were able to find other employment: "I worked as the laborer of my father without being paid. I came in his place [to the cooperative] when he couldn't work. I did not like this and went to find work that had money in it." This is not a unique situation in modern Africa and these attitudes could be attributed to capitalism and to the impact of "modern ideas." However, when examining household relations in advanced capitalist societies such as France, the role of various other factors can be seen to play a part in creating "countervailing mechanisms." Analyzing petty commodity producers in France, Winnie Lem has convincingly shown how various ideological and economic factors, such as appeals to family solidarity or threats of disinheritance, can be brought into play to maintain control over children's labor (Lem 1988, 1999). In 1983, these types of mechanisms no longer had much power in Rwanda and the organization of labor in small industries reflected this reality. Within these industries, men were obliged to enter into the complex strategies described earlier to minimize expenses, to meet market shifts, and to find labor. Critical to the effectiveness of these strategies was the capacity for households to be "self-provisioning." The majority of agricultural labor, especially in subsistence crops, is provided by women.

INDUSTRY AND AGRICULTURE: DOMESTIC RELATIONS, WOMEN'S WORK, AND THE REPRODUCTION OF LABOR

While family labor in brick and tile production was conspicuous by its absence, the role of women's labor in agriculture was crucially important for the reproduction of these enterprises. Virtually none of the small peasant producers or pieceworkers in the study gained the larger part of their livelihood in the brick and roof tile industries; rather, almost all of the households in which they lived produced the majority of foodstuffs that they consumed.[7] The provision of the majority of these subsistence foodstuffs was the responsibility of women. Peasant women did most of the heavy labor of Rwandan agriculture (Pottier and Nkundabashaka 1989). There were regional and personal differences in the amount of field labor men provide. There are men's and women's crops. Men were primarily responsible for cash crops, housebuilding, and cattle herding. Women were responsible for the production, storage, and management of all the major subsistence crops; the food preparation; the care and education of the children; the production of household articles such as mats and baskets; drawing water; and collecting firewood. If the family hired agricultural laborers, the task of supervising them would also fall on the wife.[8] However, women did most of the day-to-day work in the fields, whether for cash or subsistence crops. The surplus these women produced was critical for the operation of the small peasant industries and underwrote the reproduction of the pieceworkers in the larger industries. This section examines the development of gender relations in Rwanda and considers the role of self-provisioning in the reproduction of labor in these industries.

Land, Labor, and Gender in Rwanda

Men and women did not maintain separate fields and all crops, except coffee, were intercropped.[9] Men, however, had no fixed obligation to use the cash they earned from cash crops, or from subsistence crops that were sold, to contribute to the subsistence of the household.[10] Women complained rather bitterly that men "want to have a lot of children, but they do not care if they get fed." Whether wealthy or poor, women were responsible for the subsistence of the household, but had limited control over the cash produced by selling their surplus or gained through their wage labor. This is very different from other societies in Africa, such as in Ghana, where Anne Whitehead argues, "no other person has rights over an individual's cash income" (Whitehead 1984:105). Even closer to home, in north Kivu, James Fairhead claims "that only a husband in a very strong position of leverage would attempt to take her day labor pay from her" (Fairhead 1990:245).

In Rwanda, women could and did earn cash, but could only control small amounts of the income they generated.[11] Women who sold goods or labor tended to buy staples that could not be produced by the family, for instance, sugar, tea, oil, and occasionally bread, with their earnings rather than bring home cash. However, if the sum they gained was sufficiently large, for instance, more than the cost of small quantities of these items, they were required to turn it over to their husbands.

Despite these limitations, wealthy women lived a much more comfortable life. Wealth for both men and women meant the capacity to hire labor and not to engage in heavy physical work. Responsibility for subsistence in the case of wealthy women meant overseeing agricultural production, rather than direct labor. Rich women managed the household and supervised all domestic activities. This was also true in the colonial and late precolonial periods. Wealthy women were responsible for overseeing the husband's clients, servants, field hands, and cowherds. During the period of Tutsi rule, a tiny elite of Tutsi women acted as managers for their husbands in a larger capacity. They could administer land, command armies, and hold court in their husbands' stead. The vast majority of Tutsi women did not have this type of wealth or power (Codere 1973:246–247). After independence, the importance of ethnicity in determining the nature of women's lives diminished. Helen Codere contends, and my fieldwork confirmed, that there was "very little, if anything, to distinguish [Tutsi women] from similarly placed

Hutu women" (Codere 1973:138). In a 1973 speech, the minister of justice, Bonaventure Habimana declared that a Rwandan woman's "role as producer . . . reinforces her motherhood. Her dignity in work pays homage to her husband and reflects back on her." He concluded this paean to the exemplary wife by stating that while the Rwandan wife might be "tempted to abandon her hoe," thoughts of her children's welfare would move her to relinquish "her own endeavors" (Habimana 1973:754). The virtuous woman was, first and foremost, a good wife and mother.

In much of the literature, the contribution of Rwandan women to agriculture or to the management of men's affairs has been belittled or ignored. Authors, such as Pierre B. Gravel and Leathern Dorsey, who discuss Rwandan farmers completely ignore the fact that women do most of the farming. They talk of women "helping their husbands" (Dorsey 1983:222; Gravel 1968a:53) and performing "light duties in the fields" (Dorsey 1983:216). In his classic study of Rwanda, Jacques J. Maquet asserts that "in agricultural tasks, there [was] no specialization by sex" (Maquet 1961a:16). Even Bonaventure Habimana, who discusses the woman's role in agriculture at length, describes the division of labor in weighted terms, arguing that men do "heavy work" outside the home, while women do the "upkeep" (Habimana 1973:752). Codere provides the only countervailing voice in the earlier literature (Codere 1970:164; 1973:246–247, 250). It is only recently that authors such as Fairhead (1989, 1990, 1993), and Joachim Voss (1989, 1992) have documented the critical role of women in agriculture in the region. Voss has shown that women do most of the heavy work of field cultivation (Voss 1992). Fairhead and Voss have both documented the elaborate knowledge that women have of plant breeding for local conditions (Fairhead 1990; Voss 1989, 1992). However, this work and knowledge did not translate into power within the household. Women had limited control of the fruits of this labor within the household, and none if their husband chose to sell their produce.

CONTROL OVER WOMEN'S LABOR

Men's control over women arose from a number of interrelated factors. They maintained control over women through their children and through brideprice. Men could claim children as members of their lineage if they had paid the brideprice, in which case women had to leave their children with the husband upon separation or divorce. This was a powerful sanction for women, as Fairhead tells us, "The term *ikishingabuye* (from *gushinga ibuye*, or 'to stake a stone' . . .) refers to a woman who is stabilized in a house, thanks to her children" (Fairhead 1990:196). Violence also played a major role in a man's control over his wife/wives. Wife beating was a sign of power, and could enhance a man's reputation (Fairhead 1990:196). A woman could return to her parent's home but was unlikely to find a warm welcome since her family was responsible for repaying the bride-price, sometimes with a penalty, in the event of a split. This disincentive put enormous pressure on her to return to her husband (Fairhead 1990:195–196). When asked if their fathers or brothers would protect them or even punish their husbands for beating them, women in Rwanda frequently stated that "when you are married, it is as if you were never a member of your family, they no longer know you." As the proverbs state, *Umukŏbwa asiya zílyamiye imyugaliro akajya kuruha:* "The cow leaves the large herd to live an unhappy life," that is to say, "The daughter does not inherit from her parents, the quality of her life depends on her husband" (Crepeau and Bizimana 1979:488 #3462); or *Umugore àmenya ay'úmukazâna mü nki˘ke ntâmenya ây'ú-mukŏbwa mü mpi˘nga:* The woman hears the words of her daughter-in-law near her fence but does not hear those of her daughter near the top of the hill (Crepeau and Bizimana 1979:474 #3365).

THE IDEOLOGY OF SELF-PROVISIONING

In Rwanda, there was a strong value placed on the household producing the majority of the basic staples (beans, sorghum, sweet potatoes, and cassava) that it consumed. The capacity or incapacity to be self-provisioning was an expression of moral worth. Although fortune and misfortune of any kind are linked to moral worth, agricultural success and failure are especially important indicators (Pottier 1990:3). In 1983, almost every Rwandan household, whether rural or urban, wealthy or poor had a garden of the important foodstuffs. In wealthy homes, this garden served a largely symbolic function. It was the sign of an upstanding, obedient, and worthy wife. For the poor, this agricultural production had deeper significance:

The urban poor, like the rural poor, hold buying food to be a public admission of "poverty and therefore a source of shame. If one is not known to be reasonably well-off, then buying food is humiliating and many poor 'prefer' to go hungry instead" (Pottier 1990:3). Agricultural failure, the inability to be self-provisioning, and poverty were a source of shame. Buying food made this shame apparent: "'Shame' . . . is not a stigma attached to buying as such, but to *having* to buy. Buying becomes shameful when it signals insufficient access to land" (Pottier 1990:23). It also signaled the capacity or incapacity of a man to control his wife/wives. Agricultural success was a source of respect and pride for women, but given women's tenuous hold on the product of their labor and their responsibility for reproducing the family, it also provided a means of control over women by men. However, this emphasis on self-provisioning also acted as a check on men. Men had the right to take women's cash income, but much less right to touch their production for household consumption (Habimana 1973:751). The more labor men had put into the production process or the larger the harvest the more they could appropriate (Fairhead 1990:236). However, they could not appropriate more than the family could "spare," because then they would force the household into the shameful position of buying to make up a shortfall.

The Rwandan response to economic crises was to change consumption patterns. Men sold more of the crops that they directly controlled, such as bananas and coffee.[12] As there was no obligation on the part of the man to use this revenue in the reproduction of the household, this did not reflect badly on the family. The main staples, beans, sweet potatoes, and taro (colocasia esculenta), were women's crops. Any decision to sell them could compromise the family's capacity to be self-provisioning. Sorghum, in the form of both beer and flour, is the other main staple. It is a joint women's and men's crop, but men decided on its disposal. In crises, women also sold less of the low-value staples, such as cassava and taro, sold high-value staples, such as beans, and bought less of the "store-bought" staples, such as oil, sugar, tea, and bread.[13] The family made do on less, resorting more and more to famine foods, such as bean leaves and cassava.

Self-Provisioning and Brick and Roof Tile Makers

The men involved in this study of the brick and roof tile industries in Rwanda all lived in households that produced some agricultural products. Different crops had different purposes and meanings. In Rwanda, at this time, sorghum grains, beans, and sweet potatoes were considered the three most important and prestigious staples. Families sold these only under duress. Cassava, while it was growing in importance, was associated with poverty and had a very low status; however, it was a staple in Kivu in the Democratic Republic of Congo (then Zaire) and could be sold across the border as a cash crop by northern households. Taro was grown in small quantities as an alternative carbohydrate in the basic diet of beans and sweet potatoes in these two regions.

In the households in this study, very few of the men involved in the peasant small industries (i.e., those in Gatovu and Ngoma) sold food crops, which was very similar to the pattern of the workers in the south (Huye), while many of the men in the north (Pfunda and Gisa) sold food crops, especially sweet potatoes, sorghum grains, and beans (see table 2). Out of the 67 peasant producers in the south, 17 (25%) sold food bananas, 0 sold sorghum grain, 16 (24%) sold sweet potatoes, 7 (10%) sold beans, 12 (18%) sold cassava roots, and 3 (4%) sold taro (roots and stalks). This is very similar to the workers from the south in Huye. Out of 35, 5 (14%) sold food bananas, and 1 (2%) sold taro

TABLE 2
Informants Selling Food Crops in the South and the North

		South	South	North
Type	Crop	Gatovu and Ngoma n = 67	Huye n = 35	Pfunda and Gisa n = 39
Men's Cash Crops	Coffee*	67 (100%)	35 (100%)	11 (28%)
	Banana Beer	57 (85%)	29 (83%)	29 (74%)
Men's Food Crops	Food Bananas	17 (25%)	5 (14%)	30 (77%)
Join Men's and Women's Crops	Sorghum Beer	11 (16%)	3 (9%)	17 (44%)
	Sorghum	0 (0%)	0 (0%)	18 (46%)
Women's Food	Sweet Potatoes	16 (24%)	9 (26%)	39 (100%)
	Beans	7 (10%)	3 (9%)	38 (97%)
	Cassava	12 (18%)	6 (17%)	5 (13%)
	Taro	3 (4%)	1 (2%)	14 (36%)

*Coffee is only grown for sale and so this number represents the number of producers. All of the other crops are grown by 100% of the producers and so the figure represents the number of producers who sell their crop/product.

roots and stalks. This stands in contrast to the workers at Pfunda and Gisa in the north. Out of 39, 30 (77%) sold food bananas, 18 (46%) sold sorghum grain, 39 (100%) sold sweet potatoes, 38 (97%) sold beans, 5 (13%) sold cassava roots, and 14 (36%) sold taro roots and stalks.

All of the households sold some beer, but the differences between banana beer and sorghum beer were important. Banana beer was given as rent for fields, but was usually brewed for recreational drinking and for sale. Sorghum beer, which was frequently consumed as a breakfast food, was brewed by households on a rotating basis. In the countryside, this brewing and sharing was one of the most important reciprocal exchanges that took place at the interhousehold level. Sorghum beer was also used to recruit festive labor. These labor groups, consisting of neighbors and kin, normally provided a morning's labor and spent the afternoon drinking beer at the hosts' homes. In general, the family needed to have large fields and a substantial surplus to make use of this form of labor. In the case of these informants, therefore, the differences in beer sales also reflect affluence and poverty. The sales of banana beer were consistent across the three groups. Fifty-seven out of 67 (85%) peasant producers in the south, 29 out of 35 (83%) workers in Huye in the south, and 29 out of 39 (77%) workers in the north sold some banana beer. The sale of sorghum beer was very different. Eleven out of 67 (11%) of peasant producers in the south; 3 out of 35 (9%) workers in Huye in the south compared to 17 out of 39 (44%) in the north sold sorghum beer. This latter figure was a sign of the greater poverty of the northerners. They held less land, therefore used less festive labor, and sold more sorghum beer, a staple, than the workers in the south. Most of the workers in the south rented some land in order to grow sufficient crops. Most of the workers in the north held smaller holdings, but did not have sufficient surplus to rent land. Coffee was always grown for sale. None of the farm families consumed coffee; therefore the figures reflect the number of families that grew the crop. All of the workers in the south grew coffee, while in the north only 11 out of 39 (28%) grew coffee. This also reflected the poverty of this group and the smaller landholdings of the peasants in this region.

This same north-south disparity was seen in access to agricultural labor and underscores the figures on food sales and poverty. In Gatovu, Ngoma, and Huye, 54 out of 102 respondents (53%) hired agricultural labor, while 74 (73%) used festive labor; virtually none used exchange labor. In the north, 12 out of 39 respondents (30%) hired labor, 4 (10%) used festive labor, and 27 (68%) used exchange labor. The figures in the south indicate that most of the informants had some surplus they could use to recruit labor and rent land. In the north, the laborers had far fewer resources, and many more were reduced to selling agricultural produce, selling their own labor in agriculture and making much greater use of exchange labor rather than hired labor or festive labor. This pattern also reflects the greater disparity in landholding and the prevalence in the north of *ubukonde* land clientage relationships in which large landholders rent land to tenants on a sharecropping basis (Pottier 1990). Much more of the surplus is tied up in these relationships, allowing far less flexibility for the laborers.

This difference in land tenure, common property systems, and agricultural production between regions had important implications for both large and small brick- and tile-making industries in Rwanda, and as we will see in chapter 7, for violence in Rwanda. The capacity to be self-provisioning was critical to small peasant producers. It allowed men involved in these industries the flexibility to ride out changes in the market. Many of the smallest producers started up their enterprises with money generated through the sale of banana beer. The two common strategies used by the small peasant producers, that is, moving between wage labor, group activities, and individual labor, and combining this strategy with hiring labor, reflected the lack of extrahousehold and intrahousehold claims that could be made on labor. Within the brick and tile enterprises, men could count only on their own labor.

Within the household, men had very strong moral and coercive claims on their wives' labor and surplus, much more tenuous claims on the labor of children, and virtually no claims on the surplus generated by children after they reached puberty. Men also had the final decision-making power over what was produced and consumed by the family (Fairhead 1990; Habimana 1973:751). They could not take decisions that left the household with a severe shortage if the household was capable of being self-sufficient. However, they could influence the extent to which high-value staples were sold and replaced by low-value staples in the diet. If the household was not capable of being self-provisioning, then men also played a role in decisions to sell staples and in allocating the income. Through these mechanisms, men's industrial labor was reproduced through women's agricultural labor.

For the capitalist enterprises and for those small peasant producers who hired wage labor on a consistent basis, self-provisioning had a number of effects. It allowed these industries to run on a part-time basis and so reduced the investment necessary to operate them. It made piecework feasible, because laborers did not live on the wages they earned but lived on their wives' agricultural production; but this also made laborers less dependent on this employment income and more independent. Examining the differences between pieceworkers in the south, where most owned land and had some access to *commune* land, and in the north, where many held or rented very small plots of land and had virtually no access to *commune* land, illustrates the role of agricultural production in underwriting these enterprises and in limiting the power that owners exercised over laborers.

In the south, pieceworkers were constantly moving between employers, leaving when they were tired of the work. Very few commented on problems with the seasonality of the industries. Virtually none searched for alternative sources of cash during the rainy seasons. Laborers in the north had very different concerns. Seasonality was seen as a problem, and few men left enterprises over pay disputes. The following response was far more typical: "I quit my work here temporarily during the rainy season to go and make tiles, or to help my family cultivate. However, if the patron needs bricks and if there is some sunshine, I prefer brick making." As often as not, working in others' fields was the major alternative. These laborers were far more dependent on the wages they earned than the laborers in Ngoma, even in the industries run on the same scale. The attitude of the laborers in the north toward the role of women in "self-provisioning" was very clear: "I quit either to work my fields or because it rains and the bricks, which determine our pay, won't dry because of the effect of the rain. But the work in the fields is less important and the woman can take care of it herself, and if the rains stop I come back here to work so that I can have money." In the north, the owners were very selective, looking for laborers who were unlikely to cause trouble or leave arbitrarily. In the south, gaining access to laborers and retaining skilled laborers was a challenge and entrepreneurs needed to maintain a good reputation for paying advances or for paying on time to retain labor.

The small peasant producers in the south faced the same difficulty as the capitalist entrepreneurs. Recruiting and maintaining labor was a major problem. Wider access to clay lands allowed laborers to gain skills and to mount their own enterprises. Wider access to agricultural lands that made self-provisioning much more possible allowed these men to accumulate capital in order to do so. The capitalist entrepreneurs in the south had the capacity to control more favorable locations and to enter into larger markets but their capacity to control their labor force was more tenuous. Both groups could operate their enterprises on a seasonal basis, which reduced investment in infrastructure. In the north, laborers were not as likely to move between enterprises and were very unlikely to set themselves up as small producers. In this region, owners of enterprises did not see recruiting labor as a big problem and many entrepreneurs delayed paying laborers and did not offer advances. Moreover, they were able to work into the rainy seasons, because they had willing workers dependent on their wages. The real wage[14] paid to laborers in the brickyards was also lower when the losses to rainfall were taken into account.[15] Despite the added problems and potential losses, many laborers were prepared to take the risk.

GENDER RELATIONS, KINSHIP, AND LABOR ORGANIZATION

In Rwanda, historical processes stripped the lineage of economic, political, and social power. Kin ties did not link their members in a complex mesh of rights and obligations. Rather they became a mechanism through which clientage ties could be formed. These processes had also strongly affected the claims that kin and family members could make on one another. Parents had few structural means at their disposal to make claims on the labor of their children, especially as these children grew older. This lack of control influenced the nature of the small peasant industries in Rwanda, and led to the use of individual mixed strategies of production based on a combination of selling wage labor, hiring labor, and group production in areas of open access clay lands. However, these same changes gave men considerably more power over women's labor and production, thus freeing laborers and small peasant producers to work in a seasonal industry. The wages of laborers and the incomes of small producers did not represent the cost of the reproduction of either the worker or his family during the rainy seasons.

The capacity to be self-provisioning through women's agricultural labor, however, also provided some advantages to the laborers, especially in the south where men had access to adequate agricultural land. The labor force was less dependent on the wages they earned and so were in a good bargaining position and could change enterprises or quit temporarily if the labor conditions did not suit their needs. In the north the capitalist enterprises had a stronger hold on their workforce because of greater inequality in access to land that made many laborers only partially self-provisioning and dependent on their wages to make up the shortfall. These processes also created severe problems in the late 1980s and early 1990s when population grew markedly along with growing corruption that increased disparities in landholding dramatically (D. Newbury 1999:32; Uvin 1998:112–113). As will be shown in chapter 7, this was critical for the development of extremism in Rwanda.

For women, this role in self-provisioning, combined with the limitations placed on their capacity to control the product of their labor and their lack of access to land, goes a long way toward explaining why women were not found in the labor force of these enterprises. Peasant women had little capacity to accumulate capital, control surplus, or command productive resources and the gender division of labor and responsibility did not allow them to be self-reproducing. Women could enter into brick and roof tile enterprises only at the level of capitalist entrepreneurs. There were three women entrepreneurs in this study, but as we will see in chapter 6, the nature of Rwandan gender relations placed severe constraints on these women.

6

Loose Women, Virtuous Wives, and Timid Virgins

Class, Gender, and the Control of Resources

Three elite women owned and operated capitalist brick and roof tile enterprises in Rwanda. Their stories touched, intrigued, and puzzled me. Each presented herself and her actions, and the lives and actions of other women, in terms I found difficult to understand, in the language of stereotype and public morality. Others, both men and women, often used the same idiom to comment on or explain the problems and the attainments of these women. Some aspects of their lives seemed unique; other aspects seemed to illustrate the constraints and possibilities all Rwandan women face. As owners of capitalist enterprises these women stood in a distinct class relation to the laborers in their enterprises. However, their capacity to establish and maintain control over them differed from that of men in a similar position. This chapter examines the relationship of gender and class and the impact of this relationship on these women's everyday lives. In Rwanda, men and women had separate responsibilities for household reproduction, but men had rights over any surplus a woman might generate. Although their actions were limited because of the nature of gender relations in Rwanda, women were not passive actors in this process. There was a struggle between men and women over access to women's surplus. At the local level, the language of public morality and stereotype was one weapon in this struggle. The stereotypes of women as loose women, virtuous wives, or timid virgins were used by both men and women to interpret, manipulate, validate, or negate control over labor, resources, and surplus.

GENDER AND ACCESS TO THE MEANS OF PRODUCTION

At the commonsense level, it is clear that elite women occupy a different position and have different interests from poor women. However, difficulty arises in attempting to devise analyses that can deal with women's diverse socioeconomic and historical circumstances. Jeanne Koopman Henn argues that women form a single class, because they most often do not directly control access to critical resources (Henn 1988:27–59). However, this approach does not explain the diversity of actions and interests of women at different levels in class societies. In Henn's analysis, the capacity and willingness of elite women to exploit poorer men and women appears to arise from "false consciousness." Her contention has little explanatory value and suggests that transforming property relations will end women's oppression. Numerous critiques show how gender modifies women's class position and relationship to the state, while recognizing that different women have specific class interests (Parpart and Staudt 1989; Robertson and Berger 1986; Stichter and Parpart 1988). In one such critique, Clair Robertson and Iris Berger argue that women's class positions can be understood by analyzing direct or indirect access to critical resources. This definition, they argue, elucidates the situation of upper-class women, who, at least temporarily, control critical resources through their husbands, even if they do not directly own the means of production. In this context they assert, "it does not matter who *owns* something; more important is who can *use* and/or *control* it" (Robertson and Berger 1986:15).[1]

However, control over resources is only one aspect of the social relations of production, which can be defined "as relations which determine the forms of access to resources and the means of production, organize the labor processes, and determine the distribution and circulation of the social product of labor" (Godelier 1979:17). Control over resources is not automatically accompanied by control over the income or products generated through the use of those resources. In any given society, gender relations may affect a woman's capacity to control various aspects of the social relations of production in different ways. Both are the products of a specific history.

GENDER, THE LEGAL STATUS OF WOMEN, AND SOCIAL EXPECTATIONS IN RWANDA

Legally, married women in Rwanda had severely circumscribed rights. They could vote, but their husbands' consent was required for them to engage in commerce, register a business, buy land, act as a witness, or undertake court action.

Women could open bank accounts but husbands had the right to withdraw money from their wives' accounts without permission. By acting as "good wives," women could continue to engage in many activities and to try to retain control over their income. However, this was a "managerial" position that could not easily be transformed into a permanent capacity to control resources and surplus. It could be lost at divorce, or through the death or remarriage of the husband. A husband was well within his rights to use a wife's production to marry polygynously. He could reallocate his resources at any time, giving a prosperous business to another wife, or forbidding a wife access to her own bank account.

In theory, widows were in the best legal and social position. A widow was considered to be the head of her household, that is to say, she could attend community assemblies and speak at them. Socially, she was independent of the authority of her father, brothers, and husband for the first time. In reality, her position was still quite vulnerable. She could not sell her husband's land, although she had the right to use it if she had a son and was able to show that she could farm it. If her son was an adult, her position was secure as long as he was willing to protect her. If her son was too young to inherit, a woman could claim to be the "custodian" of his inheritance. A woman without a son had few legal and no social avenues of recourse. It was not uncommon for a young widow to be driven from her husband's land by his kin, often losing property acquired by her outside the marriage because all conjugal property was considered to belong to her husband.[2]

In principle, unmarried women had full legal status under Rwandan law; however, socially they were wards of their fathers and brothers. A woman could try to gain temporary access to her father's resources by acting in a socially acceptable fashion, as a timid virgin, whereas, a woman who was willing to flout all social conventions could become a *femme libre*, a "loose woman." These are two sharply delineated roles. Virginity, or the public show of chastity, was very important.[3] Bearing an illegitimate child classified a woman as a *femme libre* and removed any familial responsibility to provide for her and protect her. It also carried considerable social stigma and often condemned a woman to a life of prostitution.

Originally, the term *femmes libres* was "coined in the colonial Congo ... and referred to women who were legally qualified to reside in African townships ... in their own right by virtue of having their own identity card" (Obbo 1980:153). The term has grown to include "prostitutes, mistresses, concubines, temporary companions and single women indiscriminately" (MacGaffey 1988:171). Robertson and Berger argue that this role enables women to "gain access to resources but retain economic autonomy" (Robertson and Berger 1986:15).[4] As the case studies will show, being unmarried, or a wife, or a widow, and being seen either as virtuous or "loose" each provided distinct opportunities, and depending on the situation, each also created distinct limitations.

LOOSE WOMEN, VIRTUOUS WIVES, AND TIMID VIRGINS: THREE WOMEN ENTREPRENEURS

The three women in my study came to my attention for different reasons. Vestine, a young unmarried woman, was the only woman who ran a brick business in my principal field site, Gatovu. Mediatrice, a married woman, had a very forceful personality and an unusual relationship with her husband. Devota, a widow, insisted that her enterprise was run by her dead husband. They were among my best informants, willing to give detailed information and to comment on their experiences, problems, and plans. They were all entrepreneurs, and the only women directly connected with brick or tile making among the one hundred brick or tile makers interviewed.

As businesswomen, these women's practices were the same as those of the men who ran similar enterprises. Profits in the Rwandan brick and tile industries were made through the extraction of absolute surplus value. All three women paid their laborers for the number of dried bricks or tiles ready for the kiln. Using a piecework system allowed them to reduce losses in the early production stages. To decrease their expenses, they characteristically put off paying as long as possible. They were not exemplary or benevolent bosses. The following cases will show how these women acted as members of the elite, indicate how gender relations modified their class position, and then discuss the impact of different historical processes on women capacity's to act in their class position.

VESTINE

Vestine was born in 1962, and was twenty-three at the time of the interviews. She had eight years of primary school education and was unmarried. Her father was a wealthy and influential man by rural standards and he had two wives. At the time of the first interview, Vestine was still living with her mother, who was the first wife. During the course of the interviews she moved into her own home, a brick-faced building that was a combination home/shop and storehouse. She also gave birth to an illegitimate stillborn child. She was involved in many businesses. She ran a "cabaret," a bar where sorghum beer, banana beer, bottled beer, and soft drinks were sold. She bought staples such as beans, sorghum, and sweet potatoes to resell. She sold a small amount of goods, such as soap, detergent, candles, sugar, and tea in her shop. She also administered the land that her mother was allotted by her husband.[5] She hired laborers and paid them with beans and sweet potatoes to cultivate this land; she grew cash crops and rented out land to others. She also belonged to an informal cooperative that pooled money monthly and redistributed it to one member on a rotating basis. From 1983 to 1985, she ran a brick- and tile-making business.

Vestine described how and why she started this brick and tile making business when she was twenty-one years old: "I saw that those people who made bricks and tiles made a lot of money, so I decided to try it, too. In the beginning I bought unfired bricks and tiles and fired them in a kiln I had built; after, I was able to hire workers to work for me. They made the bricks and tiles and I continued to also buy unfired tiles and bricks." For a short time, she also bought fired tiles to resell but found that this was not very profitable. She did not know how to make bricks or tiles and hired laborers on a piecework basis to do this work. Hiring as many as 15 laborers at one time, she was one of the largest employers among the brick makers in the marsh. Only 4 out of 39 independent brick makers hired more than 2 to 3 laborers in this location.

The clay Vestine used came from a communal pit in the marsh. This pit was set aside by the *commune* for this purpose and it was used by almost all the people making bricks and tiles in this area. The kiln, which she owned, was built in 1983. At the time of the interviews, she rented it out to others. She bought wood from peasants who had wood lots or from government-owned stands of trees, and specialized tools from the local carpenter. Hoes she borrowed from her parents. The only factor of the means of production she was not able to control was access to clay. Government control over the clay site became crucial factor in her struggle to maintain her operation because it provided the other brick makers with the means to drive her out of business.

In 1985, the government decided that the brick and tile makers in this marsh had to join the cooperative. The cooperative had been running on and off for several years. In 1985 there was renewed pressure to make all the brick makers in the valley join. Many of the producers joined this cooperative grudgingly but, given the government control over the clay site, they had to join or stop completely. Vestine also joined at this time. She had successfully resisted doing so before, but because her brother-in-law was a founder of the cooperative and a member of the executive, she had little choice but to join. She was the only woman member of this cooperative.

She had disagreements with the other members from the beginning. Because she did not know how to make bricks, she had to hire laborers. This created problems, since the idea of the cooperative was to redistribute profits and eliminate the distinction between laborers and owners. She was told either to come and work herself or to pay higher salaries to her laborers. On the surface, this seemed in keeping with the goals of the cooperative. However, she was not the only member of the cooperative who did not know how to make bricks or tiles, or who hired laborers. Most of the members who started out not knowing how to make bricks and tiles decided to learn. However, three did not make any effort at all; Vestine was one of these three. The other two men became members of the executive, because they were from influential or affluent families. She was the only one of the three who had extra conditions attached to her membership and who became the target of public ridicule:

> I paid workers to come in my place to meet my quota to the cooperative and during firing, but the coop refused these workers. At meetings they told me to pay the workers more than the going rate. They told me I had to come and do the work myself. If I came down to the pit, they would call to me saying: "Come and work with us, strip down, it is a hot day."[6] They would jostle me. I became annoyed with the cooperative, it was too hard to work with them. They gave me extra conditions as a member, even when they hired workers to meet a big order. I decided to stop making bricks and tiles and spend more time building my own home and running my other businesses. It was tedious and unrewarding making bricks and tiles, and I make more money running my shop.

During 1985, the cooperative ran into problems as a result of which many members became increasingly discontented. The sporadic distribution of the profits, constantly changing schemes for redistributing income, disappearing funds, and the unequal commitment of different members caused considerable bad feeling among the membership. Over the year, members drifted out of the cooperative, some to set up their own kilns and some covertly to earn wages in private brickyards. Ironically, almost all the men who quit the cooperative started producing bricks and tiles independently and they continued using the public clay site. The two male members in the same position as Vestine also quit in 1985. Both men went back to running private brickyards. Vestine, forced out of the cooperative by ridicule and harassment, decided to let her tile business drop, rent out her kiln, and concentrate on her other businesses.

As an unmarried woman, Vestine had neither influence nor power in her own right. Her father, a powerful man, chose not to support her publicly. As his daughter, Vestine was able to use his resources to establish her own economic enterprises. Despite his public lack of support, he did not stop her from continuing to do so, nor had he taken control of her enterprises. He had every right to do so if he wished. Nevertheless, he risked being ridiculed if he defended her publicly. By becoming pregnant and by moving out of her mother's house, she had already shown that she was disobedient. Had she acted correctly, as a timid virgin and dutiful daughter, the cooperative members would not have dared to mock her publicly. The harassment she underwent was designed to make her leave.

There was one other case of a woman working in a brick cooperative in the adjacent *commune*, acting as secretary of the cooperative. Her husband had been working as a laborer for over a year and a half in a private enterprise ten kilometers away. She had filled his position as a member of the executive for that time without any problems. She was seen as filling her husband's position, not trying to create her own.

An unmarried woman could thrive in business. A clever young woman, such as Vestine, using her family's resources to get started, could flourish. Public morality was important, but acceptability could also be gained through a lover. Vestine would have been respected had she been publicly supported by her lover. She chose to be independent and this left her vulnerable. Marijke Vandersypen portrays a similar case, showing how precarious this route can be:

> I know a woman who, over a period of a few months, tried to earn her living completely on her own. She had a house built near her brother's house, who is a mason; she started a beer business, which quickly became successful, without becoming involved with her customers, which would have made her dependent all over again. But she was not able to hold on to this resolve for long. Those around her did not like her attempt: slandered, especially by jealous neighbors, treated as a "loose woman" by her old lovers, rejected by her brother who wished to impose his authority, she became very ill and her efforts resulted in nothing. (Vandersypen 1977:113)

The following two cases illustrate the ways in which acting as a virtuous wife can enable women to gain access to resources and to successfully run an enterprise.

Mediatrice

Mediatrice ran a large and very successful enterprise. Born in 1943, Mediatrice had had three years of secondary school that was very unusual for a woman her age. She was married and had seven children. Her husband, Christophe, had finished secondary school. Her father was a government employee in the colonial regime and in the two successive regimes after independence. Her husband's father had been a powerful landowner, in the neighboring *prefecture* where both Mediatrice and Christophe were born. They had both worked in jobs around the country, in both the government and the private sector. They moved to their present home in 1978, where they bought the land on which they lived and the land on which they established their brickyards. She was an unusually lively, outspoken, and forceful woman while her husband was a shy and quiet man.

Mediatrice and her husband were involved in a number of businesses, in addition to their brick and tile operations. They grew and sold vegetables for the market and they owned a truck and hired it out for transporting goods. Mediatrice was also employed by the *commune*, as was her oldest son. She and her husband started the brick business because they had money to invest and at the time the profits in this business were very high. Neither knew how to make bricks or tiles, although Mediatrice had learned a significant amount about the practical aspects of production at the time of the interviews. The business, started in 1982, had been so successful that they bought extra land and expanded. I interviewed her husband first, as he was ostensibly the owner of the enterprise and then interviewed Mediatrice. The difference between the two interviews was revealing.

Mediatrice's husband discussed his operation openly, and his responses showed how he viewed the ownership of various resources and the day-to-day operation. For example when he described the day-to-day problems he used the first person plural: "We have trouble finding wood, it is expensive; . . . we bought our tools at a local workshop; . . . generally, we look for contracts to sell our goods." When he discussed transporting the finished bricks, he made the following distinction: "We usually rent the trucks from the buyer but sometimes I use my own truck for transporting the bricks." When asked about the history of the enterprise and about access to resources, he asserted his claim over resources clearly: "The land is mine . . . I started with a small lot and when I saw that the business was interesting I bought more land and hired more workers." His wife, Mediatrice discussed this business in very different terms: "I'm always looking for new ways to improve the business. I find supervising the operation exhausting. The workers always cause problems. I'm thinking of trying machines, I heard that the Belgians produce some good ones, but I haven't seen anything interesting to date." She described the production process in detail, enumerated the costs, considered the economies of scale of various kilns, reviewed the problems of selling on a large scale, and assessed the pros and cons of different innovations, always using "I." However, she used "we" for discussing ownership: "We started the business in 1982 . . . it went well so we bought more land. We moved here from Kigali and bought land with our money, selling what we had in the neighboring region." As a wife, she clearly saw herself as having a joint interest in the property they had acquired and in the business she ran.

This business produced between 500,000 and 1,000,000 bricks annually. They were all sold on contract to projects and large builders. The competition for these contracts was fierce. In principle, her husband carried out all the negotiations. In reality, Mediatrice did much of the negotiating, made the contacts, and found the contracts, while her husband paid the bribes and signed the deals. Observing the day-to-day operation of this business made it clear that Mediatrice ran this enterprise and she was respected for her business acumen in the region. Her neighbors and other informants all clearly considered her to be the "boss."

Mediatrice considered herself in charge of this enterprise and to have claims over the resources she managed, while her husband considered her to be a joint manager of the venture and the resources on which it was built to be exclusively his. This assertion was also underscored by the fact that I initially interviewed him without knowing he was Mediatrice's husband.[7] No mention whatsoever was made of his wife during this first meeting; however, in subsequent meetings he referred me to his wife for details of their enterprise.

The third case is that of a widow who has translated her dead husband's power and authority into a successful small business.

Devota

Born in 1938, Devota was the oldest of the three women. Like most women her age, she had no education. She was the widow of a man who had held an important political post. In addition to running the brick making industry, Devota grew and sold a wide variety of crops, using hired labor; she owned a shop and speculated in staple crops; and she cultivated tea.[8] Arguing that her husband was "still the head of the household in this family," she discussed all aspects of her business operations as though her husband, who had been dead for more than three years at that time, were an active member of the operation: "When we know someone who is building we go and ask them to buy at our place. We don't have trucks . . . we have bricks up to two years before we sell them because there is too much competition." Like Mediatrice, she described resources as jointly owned: "The land is ours. . . . Most of it we inherited from our grandparents, but we bought some to make the parcel bigger." This last statement is very important, because Devota had brought inherited land into the marriage. It was most unusual for a woman to inherit land but she was an only child and her father was the only son in his family.[9]

In 1974, Devota and her husband started one of the very first Rwandan-owned and -operated brickyards in the valley. The scale of her business fell between those of Mediatrice and Vestine. She employed between ten and thirty employees on a seasonal basis. Her brick business had begun to suffer because of the increased competition in the valley and her tile business was underwriting her brick business. Tiles were sold to peasants, while bricks were sold to merchants, development projects, and the rich. Tile sales were less lucrative, but did not depend on connections.

Without understanding the context in which wives and widows operate one might view Devota's behavior as incomprehensible. For example, she listed her occupation as "cultivatrice" (farmer) in the same way a peasant woman would, as if she did not run a wide variety of businesses and even though she was *legally* the head of her household. Using her husband's name as head of the enterprise maintained some of his connections and some of the status associated with his political appointment. It also established her right to administer this business, to use her husband's land and resources, and to use the profits of the enterprise. By de facto characterizing her profession as one of "simple farmer" she also established her claim as a good wife and mother.

It is interesting to note that her laborers also considered her husband the owner. Even laborers hired after her husband's death considered him the head of the enterprise. Women had no trouble hiring labor in Rwanda, if they could afford it, but they did have trouble maintaining control over laborers. The involvement of a man, even if he was dead, added legitimacy to Devota's capacity to control her labor force. Acting virtuously as a widow was powerfully sanctioned in Rwanda. A widow receiving a visit from an unrelated man was often harassed or even robbed. One widow told me of being kept awake by "bandits" who sat outside her enclosure[10] and spent the night whispering that they were there to take the money that the stranger had given her, implying that the visitor had paid for sexual services. Inappropriate behavior would also give a widow's husband's kin grounds to seize her property.

CLASS AND GENDER IN RWANDA

All three women's control over resources and surplus arose out of the one-to-one relationship they had with influential men. In the precolonial kingdom, many men gained access to the means of production through dyadic ties and not through lineage ties. The loss of lineage rights placed women in a position where they gained the right to use the means of production only through men and they lost the right to control any surplus. In contemporary Rwanda, women's wealth and power were defined by the position of their husbands, lovers, or fathers. However, like the patron-client tie between men, the degree of control a woman had over resources and surplus was an expression of a particular man's confidence in a particular woman's abilities. Women could, by indirect means, gain considerable power and enjoy substantial wealth. However, they could not easily safeguard that position.[11]

In a number of African states, such as Uganda or the Democratic Republic of Congo, women did not have clear legal protection over their rights and properties. In a number of others, the reinterpretation of "customary law" had eliminated preexisting rights. Nonetheless, as numerous West African cases show, women can and do still act on informal rights they possess. Much of the discussion of gender relations in Africa is based on this fact. In Rwanda, women had great difficulty laying social claims to rights under the law, because they had few social rights under customary law.

In Ghana, Penelope Roberts argues, men defer "paying" women for their labor or increasing the productivity of women's farms, "since the attainment of a small income . . . is sufficient for many women to separate from or divorce their husbands" (Roberts 1988:109). In comparison, Janet MacGaffey specifically addresses the rights a man and his kin could have in a wife's business in the Democratic Republic of Congo. She states that "property resulting from the profits of petty trade can be seized by the husband's kin, if the husband gave his wife a small sum of money to begin her trading career" (MacGaffey 1988:161–176, esp. 164). Women in Rwanda also could not translate the temporary right to control resources and surplus into permanent control because they could lose any property, income, or enterprise on the same grounds.

These women were able to establish enterprises and to exploit the labor of poorer men because they were able to control scarce resources. However, their capacity to maintain this position was negotiated through their public roles as wives, daughters, and lovers of the men who legally owned the enterprises and who had claims over the resources and the surplus they generated. The development of wage labor in precolonial Rwanda freed labor from the institutions that often make it difficult for women to gain access to labor in other African societies. Ironically, the same historical processes that enabled these elite women to gain access to, and control over, cheap labor had also removed women's control over their own surplus. They had no publicly recognized right over their resources and surplus beyond the personal relationships they had established with powerful men.

This had peculiar implications for the genocide, which will be discussed in chapter 7, but it bears discussing here because of the nature of this link between clientage and power in elite women's relations to elite men. Marriage to elite Hutu women was considered important for the mobility of Hutu elite men, especially in the north, but elite Tutsi women were considered much more beautiful. There was a phenomena of Hutu elite men, especially for members of the military who were forbidden to marry Tutsi women, of marrying a Hutu wife and taking a Tutsi mistress. In addition to this phenomena, in the south where intermarriage was less stigmatized, elite Hutu men frequently married Tutsi women or Hutu women who matched the Tutsi stereotype, leaving a group of elite Hutu women who felt passed over. This created a considerable ethnic tension among elite women and may have led to the number of elite Hutu women who were implicated in the genocide.[12] Others, such as the minister for women and family affairs, Pauline Nyiramashuhuko, appears to have been motivated by politics and ambition. More commonly, women were active in the looting during the genocide and did not engage in the killing on anywhere near the same scale as men.

7

Brickyards Turn to Graveyards

In April 1994, these brickyards changed to graveyards in a state-sponsored genocide that killed approximately five hundred thousand Rwandans, both Tutsi and the moderate Hutu.[1] Two thirds of the population was scattered across the region, either as internally displaced in Rwanda or as refugees in the other countries of the Great Lakes region. Tens of thousands were turned into killers by a genocidal Hutu extremist government and many thousands died in the war that reerupted. The media have emphasized the role of ethnicity and ethnic politics in these events and imbued them with an air of inevitability as one more example of "tribal violence" in Africa. A closer look shows that the factors that made the genocide possible are more complex and less inevitable than these reports would suggest. Economic recession, economic restructuring, population growth, patterns of elite access to power, regional politics, civil war, "democratization," the politics of other countries of the Great Lakes region, and international policies all played a role in the move to the genocide. This chapter will examine the background to the genocide, consider the role that class and regional differences played in the spread of the genocide across the country, and end with a look at the current regime. I will argue that the factors that conditioned the development of these small industries—the centralization of power; the transformations in land tenure and access to resources; regional disparities; and the growth of self-interested elites; coupled with war, economic crisis, and structural adjustment, were also the factors that underlay the politics of the 1994 genocide, and are the factors that have driven the politics of Rwanda since 1994.

BACKGROUND TO THE GENOCIDE

From the mid-1980s on, the economic growth that Rwanda had experienced in the 1970s and early 1980s under the Habyarimana regime slowed dramatically[2] and by 1989, after the dramatic fall in coffee prices, Rwanda's principal export, the regime was faced with the need to restructure its economy. The same period saw growing corruption of functionaries and an increasing distance of these functionaries from the predominantly rural population (C. Newbury 1992). The main benefits of the state, access to land, power, education, and jobs, were concentrated into the hands of a smaller and smaller elite within the government, at a time during which population growth and ecological decline placed increasing pressure on these resources (D. Newbury 1999). The 1989 fall in coffee prices brought this economic crisis to a head. Coffee prices fell by 50% in 1989 and hundreds of thousands of households lost 50% of their cash income because coffee was a small holder crop. The economic restructuring that followed, through an IMF (International Monetary Fund) structural adjustment program, caused food prices to soar, salaries to fall, public services to collapse, and led to a 40% devaluation of the Rwandan franc (Chossudovsky 1995a; C. Newbury and D. Newbury 1994:1; Olson 1994:4). Several areas of the country suffered a drought and, for the first time since independence, people could not afford to buy food, emergency stocks were reduced, and people died of hunger (C. Newbury 1992; C. Newbury and D. Newbury 1994).

During this period, on October 1, 1990, the Rwandan Patriotic Front (RPF) invaded Rwanda. The Rwandan army was totally unprepared and the RPF almost made it to Kigali. They were beaten back only by the intervention of Rwandan, Belgian, and French troops. The government used this opportunity to jail its enemies, Tutsi and Hutu (Human Rights Watch 1999a), and to increase political repression in the country. Economically, the war funneled most of the available resources and aid money into arms and expanding the army, which grew from 5,000 to 50,000 during the years that followed (Human Rights Watch/Africa 1999a; Uvin 1998), and arms flooded the country.

At the same time, the population bomb exploded. There was little land for the new cohort of youth reaching the age of majority in an economy that remained based on agriculture and in which few nonfarm options existed or had been created. From the 1940s to the mid-1980s, new lands were opened up and this helped deal with the population pressure, but by the 1980s "these options were virtually exhausted" (Olson 1994:4). There was no new land to be opened up and farm sizes shrank to an average of 0.7 hectares. These young men had nothing to inherit and had few nonfarm options. Until the economic restructuring, Habyarimana's regime had provided a few rural-based projects to absorb some of these youth, but even these relatively ineffectual efforts disappeared with restructuring. Peasants also lost access to health care, schooling, and other services that had been subsidized by the state, while the elites took advantage of the new opportunities that restructuring presented.

Amid this economic and political crisis the rich became much richer. Prominent among the richest of the rich were the military, government officials, and the supporters of Habyarimana, most of whom were drawn from the north of Rwanda (Reyntjens 1994:33–34). Every region saw the growth of an elite that had fewer and fewer connections with the peasantry (C. Newbury 1992), and increasingly this elite openly disparaged the rural and poor (Uvin 1998:129). Emergency land sales skyrocketed, and land concentration escalated (Uvin 1998:112–113). While 86% of the population lived below the poverty line, the income share of the wealthiest decile of the population increased from 22% in 1982 to 52% in 1994 (Uvin 1998:115). One informant summed up this transformation succinctly when he said, "We, the elites, were so comfortable in those last years, running after the new things we could have for the first time, that we forgot about the problems of the poor."

The late 1980s and early 1990s saw a heightening of political opposition and calls for democratization, as well as growing criticism in the international community of the Habyarimana regime. The world community responded to the criticism by pushing for democratization (Human Rights Watch/Africa 1999; Uvin 1998). However, this push did not lead to a real opening up of the political processes; rather it "facilitated an expansion of the elite class within the closed arena of national politics." Catherine Newbury and David Newbury argue that "substantive democracy in any meaningful sense was not at issue," despite popular involvement in pushing for transition (C. Newbury and D. Newbury 1996:2, 9). Because of structural adjustment, even those elites interested in pushing for reforms had little control over the means to meet the expectations of the populace (C. Newbury and D. Newbury 1996:9).

The civil war also played an important role in this lack of resources. Most of the resources were funneled into the hands of the military and their hardcore allies within the government, the two groups most resistant to democracy (C. Newbury and D. Newbury 1996:8). The transition government, put into place in 1992, did nothing to change the nature of political power in Rwanda, with new elites simply being co-opted by this system. However, it did lead to an increase in popular dissatisfaction and popular disaffection with the ruling elites. This led to a greater pillaging of the economy, greater debt, and more disparity while the war helped fuel the "ethnic" rhetoric of the extremist parties. The growth of these parties under international pressure and scrutiny also gave the opposition a false sense of security in an atmosphere of economic crisis and extremism. An informant commented bitterly, "All that multipartyism did was write the death lists." Like many political demagogues before them, Habyarimana, his regime, and other factions of the elite dealt with the unemployment crisis by arming this mass of disaffected youth. For a select group of youth, membership in the militias meant an income, power, and a place to belong (Human Rights Watch 1999a; Wagner 1998).

As discontent with the Habyarimana regime grew, so did the government propaganda, which stressed the fact that the Tutsi were the enemy and the ancient oppressors of Rwanda. The period between 1990 and 1994 saw the development of racist propaganda that made the genocide possible. The press, radio, and television propaganda featured the manipulation, simplification, and reduction of history, reducing ethnicity and politics of Rwanda to ethnic politics. These media contributed to the evolution of a "logic of genocide" to rationalize the dictatorship of President Juvenal Habyarimana, and entrenched the power of a small segment of the elite associated with this regime (Chrétien et al.1995).

In addition to this volatile blend of civil war, economic crisis, and elite politics, events in Burundi provided fuel for the propaganda machine. Independence in Rwanda and Burundi saw the growth of a "perverse dialectic" between events in Rwanda and Burundi (Lemarchand 1994a:30). Bishop André Sibomana, the courageous journalist and human rights activist, has decribed this relationship well. Burundi, he says is "a wound we [the Rwandans] have to live with, just as Rwanda is a wound for Burundi. . . . It would be wrong to say that they are similar. The mutual influence of the two countries only seems to come into play to aggravate the situation" (Sibomana 1999:149). The systematic killings of Hutu intellectuals in 1972 by a Tutsi-led exclusionary government, combined with the killings of Hutu by another Tutsi-dominated government in 1988, plus the assassination of the first elected Hutu Burundian president, Melchior Ndadaye, by a Tutsi-dominated army, were critical to the capacity of Rwandan extremists to incite fear. These events also helped the extremists to discredit the Arusha accords, the peace negotiations between the government of Habyarimana and the RPF in 1992 and 1993, in the eyes of the population. In particular, the decision to integrate the two armies with a 60/40 split in favor of the government and a 50/50 command split, which extended to the level of field commanders, and the exclusion of the extremist political faction, the Coalition pour le Défense de la République (CDR), from the negotiations proved to be disastrous. These elements hardened the extremist position and alienated the army (Jones 1999a:69, 1999b:139). The structure of the transitional government created by the Arusha accords, Filip Reyntjens argues, meant that the former government would have a difficult time mustering sufficient opposition votes to support any policy it might put forward (Reyntjens in Jones 1999b:139). Bruce Jones calls the Arusha accords "a victor's deal" because the RPF were able to impose these conditions on the then government of Rwanda, despite the advice of members of the international community. He contends that this was a hollow victory because it pushed the terms of the agreement well beyond what was acceptable to the government and to the extremist factions associated with it, without defusing those factions. This meant that they had nothing to lose by undermining the process (Jones 1999b:149–150). The killing of Ndadaye enabled the Rwandan government to challenge the tenability of the agreement and helped fuel the propaganda campaign.

Anti-Tutsi sentiment could also be manipulated so successfully because of the precolonial and colonial history of Rwanda and the makeup of the Rwandan Patriotic Front that was predominantly Tutsi. Some were drawn from the descendants of the aristocrats and their dependents who fled Rwanda from 1959 to 1963, and some drawn from the commoners and aristocrats who fled the broader-based persecutions of 1963 onward. The regime fostered by the Belgians was very rapacious, very corrupt, and linked to a racist ideology that excluded the majority of Hutu from power, access to education, and the benefits of state clientage.[3] The majority of the peasantry was terrified by the prospect of the return of this form of rule. The RPF did little to allay these fears. In their 1993 offensive, when they came within 40 kilometers of the capital, Kigali, they drove 700,000 predominantly Hutu peasants out of some of the most densely populated areas of the north and into Kigali and the south, in order to put pressure on the Habyarimana regime (C. Newbury and D. Newbury 1996:11). This expulsion provided a propaganda coup for the Habyarimana regime and "undermined the efforts of RPF to present itself as a political movement committed to gaining the confidence of the population and interested in the welfare of the population" (C. Newbury and D. Newbury, forthcoming:11). Even though there was no evidence that they had any intention of reinstating a "feudal state" as the anti-Tutsi propaganda incessantly stated, the RPF by its actions fed into the fears of the peasantry.

This fear, which had been fed by the racist propaganda of the regime during the 1990s in the journals, newspapers, and through the quasi-private radio and television station, Radio-Télévision Libre Milles Collines (RTLM), was intensified by events in Burundi, despite the fact that the vast majority of the Tutsi in Rwanda were poor peasants living in equivalent circumstances as their neighbors. The Habyarimana regime responded to the various crises it faced and the civil war was a deliberate use of ethnic violence for political ends. The killings were ordered from above. They were state-sponsored and backed by a power group of the military. Although a horrendous number were carried out by civilians, the majority were carried out by the militias (African Rights 1994; Human Rights Watch/Africa 1994a:2–7; Human Rights Watch/Africa 1999a; Mujawamariya 1994:36–52; Reyntjens 1994:298–299).[4] However, this reality disguises the extent to which the genocide, depending on political leadership, local class relations, and local history, did not follow the same pattern throughout Rwanda.

POLITICS, GENDER, CLASS, HISTORY, AND REGIONAL DIFFERENCES IN THE GENOCIDE

When Habyarimana's airplane went down on April 6, 1994, a number of things happened or did not happen: (1) most of the military stayed in its barracks waiting for the RPF; (2) the Presidential Guard and the Interahamwe (the Movement Révolutionaire pour le Développement [MRND]/CDR militias) went out to kill the opposition (the majority of whom were Hutu), the critics of the government (the majority of whom were Hutu), and Tutsi leaders; (3) other landless youth and the urban poor went rampaging through the wealthy Kigali neighborhoods; and (4) only some regions of Rwanda responded to the command to start killing. If we consider the development of the genocide throughout the country in the 1991–1993 period and in 1994, we will see that the violence was neither spontaneous nor the result of "ancient hatreds." The killings did not erupt throughout the whole country; instead, many regions stayed calm through weeks of bloodshed. The killings, where they took place, were orchestrated by various elites and targeted different groups with different degrees of success throughout the country. Each region and areas within each region either resisted or became involved for different reasons. The genocide was only the last of a series of attempts to incite ethnic violence in Rwanda but, as in the case of the Kayabanda regime in 1973, these first attempts met with limited success.

Looking at the pattern of killings in the period between 1991 and 1993, it can be seen that the major ethnic/political massacres and attacks were concentrated in Gisenyi, Ruhengeri, and Kibuye. In the genocide of 1994, we see a similar pattern. The killings in Gisenyi, Ruhengeri, and Cyangugu began almost simultaneously with the killings in Kigali. Soon after, Kibuye began the massacres. Kibungo and Gikongoro were the scenes of some of the most horrific killings during the genocide. The Bugesera region in Kigali *prefecture* also had major massacres. Butare and Gitarama were effectively left alone between 1991 and 1993 and resisted the call for the genocide the longest (African Rights 1994:583–590; Mujawamariya 1994:6–9, 25–26, 43–44, 51; Pottier and Wilding 1994:23; Reyntjens 1994:183–192, 295–297). If we consider the social, historical, and political context of this crisis region by region we can see that ethnic hatred was not the major factor in the pattern of complicity and resistence.

The North: Fictions of Tradition

By the 1980s the main positions in Habyarimana's regime, as well as access to resources such as scholarships, common property, and development aid, were concentrated in the hands of elites from the *prefectures* of Ruhengeri and Gisenyi (Reyntjens 1994:33–34). By April 1994 power was concentrated even further into the hands of certain members of Mme Agathe Habyarimana's family and certain members of the northern elite, the infamous *akazu* (little house) (Reyntjens 1994:189). At the same time, this area had one of the highest population densities in Rwanda, the greatest disparity in landholdings, and a growing landless group. The land clientage at the root of this disparity was justified as a "Hutu institution" predating Tutsi and colonial rule (Pottier 1990:3, 6–7). This area also had the lowest proportion of Tutsi in the country, because it had been incorporated into the precolonial state only during the last years of the nineteenth century (Des Forges 1986; C. Newbury 1988; Vansina 1962). The problem of landlessness and the growing gap between rich and poor made this area potentially the most explosive for the Habyarimana regime. The core of the extremists came from this area, and this extremism favored the interests of the political elite. As map 4 shows, there was a pattern of "ethnic" massacres through this area during the 1990s. In April 1994, this area helped provide manpower to help hunt down and kill Tutsi in other regions of the country (African Rights 1994; Human Rights Watch/Africa 1994:4; Mujawamariya 1994).

THE EAST: THE CONTESTED FRONTIER

The regions of Kibungo and the Bugesera in Kigali *prefecture* also saw some of the worst killing before and during the early part of the genocide. These areas were not as populated as either the northern *prefectures* or the *prefectures* of Butare and Gitarama; however, they were a major area of in-migration and the site of much of the unsettled land in Rwanda before the 1990s (African Rights 1994; Olson 1994:4; Reyntjens 1994:184). Many of the Tutsi who fled the persecutions and killings of 1959–62, 1963, and 1973, settled into this area. During the 1980s and 1990s, many of the landless and jobless youth from the north moved into these areas looking for land. By the 1980s most of the unsettled land was settled and this region could no longer absorb surplus population. During the 1990s the old established Tutsi and the in-migrant Hutu groups clashed for access to land and for power, as can be seen from map 4. Given this situation, the government targeted this area for extremist propaganda and for its campaign of killings in the 1990s, and found fertile ground among the landless youth from the north for the militias (Mujawamariya 1994:43–44, 51–52; Reyntjens 1994:184–187).

THE SOUTHWEST: NEGLECTED TERRAINS

Cyangugu in the southwest of Rwanda also was the site of killings in 1991–1993. There were also attempts to incite violence in 1991–1992 in Gikongoro but these were less successful.[5] However, after October 1993 when Melchior Ndadaye was killed in Burundi, this changed and there were massacres in

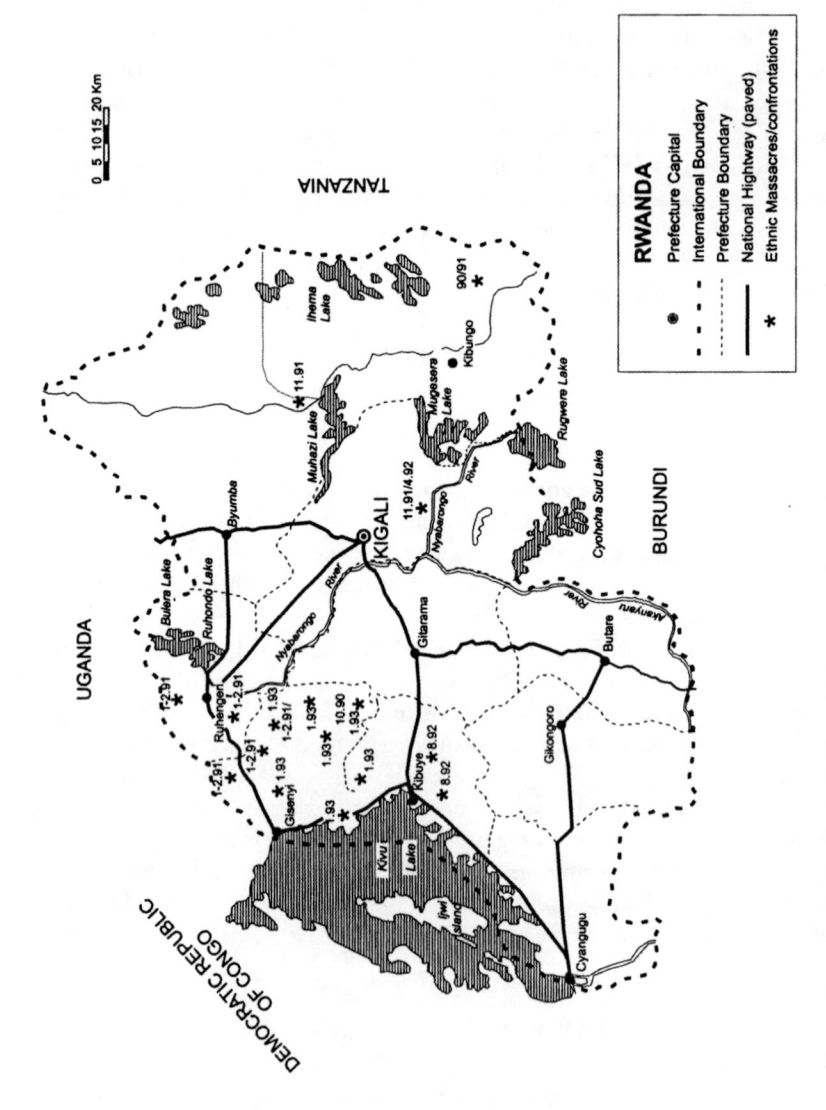

MAP 4. Rwanda. Principal Ethnic/Political Massacres or Attacks (1991–1993). Reprinted from Reyntjens (1994:186).

these *prefectures* (Reyntjens 1994:186–187). The prefect (governor) of Cyangugu, Emmanuel Bagambiki, had been implicated in massacres of Tutsi in Bugesera in 1992 and 1993 and had been involved in the killings of both Tutsi and Hutu opposition members in Cyangugu during 1993. As soon as Habyarimana's airplane was shot down, the killings began in both *prefectures* (African Rights 1994:227–231). The west of Cyangugu, near the Zaïrian border, was the worst area for killing outside of Kigali in the first days. As in the rest of the country, the witnesses interviewed in both *prefectures* dwelt on the role of extremist politicians, government functionaries, militias, soldiers, and police in leading the killings (African Rights 1994:227–231, 289–292). The "ancient hatreds" argument holds little water in this region; as Newbury documents, it was an area where the old Tutsi state had not consolidated power (C. Newbury 1988). Johan Pottier has suggested that the government fostered extremist politics and appointed an extremist *préfet* because of the strategic location of Cyangugu. It sits on a major route out of the country (Pottier 1995, personal communication).

Gikongoro was a site of the "earliest as well as some of the worst massacres in the genocide" (Human Rights Watch 1999a:303). The Human Rights Watch authors emphasize that the *prefecture* was created after independence by linking Tutsi-dominated areas with an area of highlands populated by Hutu that had had Tutsi-dominated political rule imposed during the European colonial period, making this region both volatile and lacking in history and cohesiveness. It was an area neglected by both of the republics; few of the resources of the state and the development apparatus were available to the inhabitants. It was also an area of poor soils and extreme poverty, even in a country marked by pervasive poverty. It was also an area that saw a huge influx of Burundian refugees after the assassination of the Burundian president, Ndadaye, which further radicalized the local population (Human Rights Watch/Africa 1999:303–304).

The political record during the genocide was very mixed. Although the MRND, Habyarimana's party, was very unpopular in this area, nevertheless there were two powerful men able to force a quick response to the call for the extermination of the Tutsi. The MRND prefects and a number of majors, who held power under the genocidal regime, however, tried to mitigate these policies ineffectually (Human Rights Watch/Africa 1999a:303–352). This area was ripe for violence and easily found recruits for the militias and killing parties among the poor and the refugees. These groups were used to "export" violence into the regions of Gitarama and Butare, which were resisting the order to kill (Human Rights Watch/Africa 1999a:313, 331). Political neglect and poverty played a powerful part in ensuring complicity with the genocide in Gikongoro. The anti-Tutsi rhetoric and policies of the interim government found fertile ground in this *prefecture*.

THE CENTER AND SOUTH: THE CORE OF THE KINGDOM

If the "ethnic violence" and "ancient hatreds" arguments are to be born out, then the center of the old kingdom, the *prefectures* of Butare and Gitarama should have shown the greatest degree of violence. However, this was the area that most strongly resisted the orders to kill[6] during the first weeks of the genocide. Nor did it have any ethnic or political clashes in the 1991–1993 period (see map 4). It took until April 18, 1994 for the killings to start and, in the end, the Interahamwe and presidential guards had to be brought in from Kigali and the north to force people to kill. Butare and Gitarama were the center of opposition to the northern-dominated government, and the local government was dominated by opposition members, with the notable exception of certain *communes* (African Rights 1994:583–590, 231–232, 248; Human Rights Watch/Africa 1999a; Mujawamariya 1994). There was more intermarriage between Tutsi and Hutu, and much more contact between ethnic groups. Survivors spoke of the solidarity between Hutu and Tutsi, which needed to be destroyed in order that the killings could be effected (African Rights 1994:583–584; Human Rights Watch/Africa 1999a; Mujawamariya 1994). This solidarity, coupled with opposition to the killings by the prefect, meant that even extremist politicians and Interahamwe in the *communes* were unable to act effectively on the orders to kill, although there were pockets of violence throughout the *prefecture*. It was only when the prefect was killed by the army that the broad-based killings began. Again, the political opposition, the people who refused to give the orders, or those who helped Tutsi escape, were hunted down and killed along with the Tutsi (African Rights 1994:583–590, 231–258, 607–610; Human Rights Watch/Africa 1999a; Mujawamariya 1994).

VIOLENCE AND POLITICAL MANIPULATION

The orchestrated nature of the killings is shown graphically in the statements collected by African Rights (1995) and Human Rights Watch/Africa (1999a). These statements also show how various Hutu functionaries tried to stop the killings only to be overridden and often killed (African Rights 1994:231–253, 607–617). More than anything, this ethnic violence represented a struggle between elites, as Josephine Mukandori, a survivor, tells us,

> In our sector [Kareba, Butare] and . . . in Ntyazo [Butare], Tutsis and Hutus fought together. . . . The Hutus who really fought on our side were the ordinary people, not the educated ones. . . . These ones who understood the politics of the attacks explained to the ordinary Hutus what was taking place and they began to desert us. (African Rights 1994:248)

She argues that the local population was able to hold out against the Interahamwe because the militias were armed only with machetes and clubs. The Interahamwe were able to start killing only once the soldiers arrived.

Throughout the country the so-called spontaneous violence can be shown to have been systematic and cold-blooded. It did not arise out of ancient hatreds but through overt political manipulation, ruthlessly orchestrated by a morally bankrupt elite. Factors such as the growing landlessness, disparities between rich and poor, the ambitions of an increasingly ruthless elite losing their grip on power, regional politics, and regional dynamics played a central role in the genocide and political slaughter. There is no doubt there was a difference in how Hutu and Tutsi were treated—nonpolitical Hutu were terrorized while nonpolitical Tutsi were killed—but, as Filip Reyntjens argues, the socioeconomic aspects of the killings also should not be ignored (Reyntjens 1994:299).[7] As the killings gained momentum, the violence became more complex and less linked to purely political ends. There was outright robbery (African Rights 1994:577–583). Personal vendettas were settled. Property under dispute could be appropriated by one claimant from another on the basis of accusations (Human Rights Watch 1999a; Reyntjens 1994:299). Human Rights Watch/Africa points out repeatedly that political authorities needed to chastise the mobs for looting without killing. People who had excited the jealousy of their neighbors by being marginally more affluent were attacked. As Josephine Mukandori tells us; "in the end the population lost" (African Rights 1994:248).

The world community was not immune to political manipulation and proved incapable of responding to the growing violence in Rwanda from 1990 to 1994. From 1990 onward, the regime of Habyarimana targeted Tutsi civilians for death and detainment, and the world community was loath to intervene or to impose sanctions on the government. While pressing for political and economic reforms in Rwanda, the international community accepted the continuation of human rights abuses as "necessary" to redress past injustices, the explanation of assassinations as "accidents" suffered by opposition members or critics of the regime, or the government-organized massacres of Tutsi as "spontaneous and uncontrollable" acts of violence in a situation of civil war (Human Rights Watch 1999a:17). During this time, the international community criticized the Habyarimana regime for these abuses for a brief period, but quickly went back to funding the regime and ignoring its excesses (Uvin 1998). The French were most culpable in this process. They actively funded the military and the training of the militias, even when there was considerable evidence of abuses, thereby creating the illusion of legitimacy for government actions and "major disincentives" for the regime to look for conciliation in the Arusha negotiations (Lemarchand 1994b:603).

The world community, and especially the UN, must be condemned for its negligence during the build up to the genocide and during the genocide itself. From November 1993 until April 1994, there was clear evidence that there was a genocide being planned by a faction linked to the Habyarimana regime. The most unmistakable was the December 1993 letter from high-ranking military officers to Gen. Romeo Dallaire, the head of the UN peacekeeping mission in Rwanda, showing the existence of the Reseau Zéro, of arms caches, and of a plan for mass killings. Although he reported this information to the UN on January 11, 1994 in a telegram to his superiors, he was ignored and the information was kept from the Security Council. Human Rights Watch/Africa, however, documents a far wider range of indicators, from warnings from the church to the "public incitations to murder" on the radio and in the press to the reports by intelligence officers of secret meetings in which attacks on Tutsi were coordinated. The authors of *Leave None to Tell the Story* argue that the United States, the Belgians, and most probably the French feared the possibility of mass violence and of genocide (Human Rights Watch/Africa 1994:18–19). Despite these indicators the world community was reluctant to act.

It was during the implementation of the genocide that the world community proved to be the most indecisive and remiss. The incontrovertible evidence of systematic killing of Tutsi and of Hutu opposition members was ignored. Instead the early reports described the situation as chaotic and confusing, emphasizing that the killings were the results of an "age-old tribal conflict," and UN Secretary-General Boutros-Ghali piously intoned that Rwanda had "fallen into calamitous circumstances" (Human Rights Watch/Africa 1994:20, 628). During the first days, the Presidential Guard and the *Interahamwe* killed as many of the enemies on their lists as they could find, and effectively immobilized the UN peacekeeping troops by brutally killing the ten Belgian peacekeepers guarding Agathe Uwilingiyimana, the southern Hutu prime minister. Two thousand-plus peacekeepers were withdrawn from Rwanda. This gave the extremists carte blanche to hunt down and kill opposition members and Tutsi in Kigali. The UN redefined its mission as one to protect its soldiers from harm, and the rest of the world intervened only to save their nationals (Barnett 1997). Although the original mandate called for the UN peacekeepers to protect civilians, this responsibility was quickly jettisoned. The UN would not go so far as to remove the Rwandan representative from the Security Council, even when it became evident that the government that he represented was engaged in the mass slaughter of its civilians (Human Rights Watch 1999a:17). The United States forbade its officials to use the word *genocide* in connection to the killings (Human Rights Watch 1999a:19–20). The effect of this indecision was that the interim government was able to give the impression of acting legitimately. When the world community found its voice and began to timidly criticize the actions of the interim government, the interim government restricted and hid the killings (Human Rights Watch 1999a:24–27).

THE RWANDAN PATRIOTIC FRONT AND POSTGENOCIDE RULE

While the world community wrung its hands, the Rwandan Patriotic Front quickly rekindled the civil war, and won within three months. The new regime had to establish legitimacy in the eyes of the population and the world community. Habyarimana and Kayibanda could lay claim to leading the natural majority *(rubanda nyamwinshi)* because they were Hutu. The Belgians could justify supporting the aristocratic class of the Tutsi on the basis of a racial ideology that portrayed them as "natural rulers." Ironically, in each of these cases, the international community found these arguments convincing long after the local population had grown disenchanted.

NEW GOVERNMENT, OLD PATTERNS OF RULE: FICTIONS OF HISTORY, ETHNICITY, AND GOVERNANCE

The anti-Tutsi propaganda campaign, the genocide itself, the character of the civil war from 1991 to 1994, the nature of both the ex-government *and* RPF strategies in the civil war, and the new regime's actions have made the consolidation of legitimacy a formidable challenge for the RPF. The majority of the Rwandan Patriotic Front consists of returnees, born or raised abroad. Many are descended from the old aristocracy and most of them are Tutsi. They took over a country that is wary of outsiders and in which the anti-Tutsi propaganda of the Kayibanda and Habyarimana regimes has created a peasantry that is suspicious of their motives. The events in Burundi have only exacerbated this situation. Moreover, in the first few months of their regime the world community was cautious about investing in the rebuilding of Rwanda, given the manipulations of the previous regimes. The new government was faced with the need to gain legitimacy in the eyes of the international community and the local population. While the world community quickly became enamored of the new government in power, within Rwanda the regime has faced a difficult job. Like the previous regimes it has chosen to manipulate the ideology of ethnicity rather than to work toward reconciliation.

Proponents of the first position claim that the categories of Hutu, Tutsi, and Twa are meaningless colonial and postcolonial constructions, and that there are no ethnic differences; rather, these terms are misunderstood class terms. The following assertion, in this case made by an RPF captain is typical: "If you have more than 10 cows you can become a Tutsi.... Hutu simply means 'servant' in our language. Somebody with lots of cows has the right to have servants. Tutsi just means rich" (Mudenge, interview, *Guardian*, March 5, 1994, quoted in Pottier 1995:9). Mahmood Mamdani argues that many in the current government make this statement to deny that the term *Tutsi* ever had any ethnic connotation (Mamdani 1996:6).

Proponents of the second position claim that these categories represent a precolonial reciprocity, arguing that the precolonial state was equitable and balanced, and that the exploitative elements entered it only under colonialism.[8] Research on the history of precolonial Rwanda illustrates that social relations and ethnicity underwent a radical transformation over a few hundred years, and the colonial and postcolonial states transformed both social relations and ethnicity again, first under the Germans and the Belgians, and then under the "Hutu" republics. This process of the redefinition of ethnicity continues under the RPF government. They have banned the use of ethnic terms, but this does not mean that ethnicity is no longer a factor in the formation of identity or exclusion in Rwanda.

Many Hutu remain skeptical about the equation of lack of ethnic terminology with the lack of ethnic discrimination; this skepticism is based on events in Burundi and on the nature of RPF rule. In Burundi, the lack of reference to ethnicity has not mean that one ethnic group does not continue to hold power, that ethnic discrimination is not a part of everyday life, or that the lack of overt ethnic labels have stopped the Burundian Tutsi-dominated army from massacring Hutu civilians (Lemarchand 1994a:10). In Rwanda, the current regime's commitment to transforming ethnic relations is questionable, even if the example of Burundi is discounted. Far from moving beyond ethnic labels, the RPF has conflated the term *Hutu* with *genocidaire*, and rationalized the exclusion of Hutu who are not part of the RPF from negotiations on the basis that they are all *genocidaires* (Gourevitch 1998:272, 340, 346, 350; Wagner 1998:26). Typical of this attitude is the statement of an RPF advisor who argues that "every other Rwandan Hutu [is] guilty" on the basis of the film footage he has seen (Gourevitch 1998:244). Commonly, any attempt to point out that Hutu saved Tutsi leads to the argument that the killers picked favorites and that this should not be seen as an act of heroism.[9] Most worrying is the tendency to pick and choose those to be defined as survivors (Gourevitch 1998:131; Wagner 1998:25). The process of demonizing the enemy, which permeated the hate propaganda of the extremists, continues under the new regime. Only the label has changed; now the enemy is the Hutu.

One of the eternal patterns of Rwandan politics is that elements of the elite, through their excesses, have laid the foundations for the regimes that follow to justify their own counterexcesses. This applies to the Tutsi aristocratic elite who benefited from colonial rule, as well as to the corrupt central Rwandan Hutu who benefited from the First Republic (1961–1973), and the extremist northern Hutu who benefited from the Second Republic (1973–1994). In each case, once in power, they have extended the "sins" to include a whole ethnic group on the basis of the actions of a tiny minority. The Tutsi who died in the genocide were not responsible for the previous excesses of a Tutsi minority, most of whom are long dead. They were not responsible for the fluctuations of the market for coffee, the exactions of structural adjustment, or the need of Habyarimana and his extremists to hang on to power at any cost. The Tutsi as a group were never a threat to the state, but men, women, and children, young and old, died in 1963, 1973, and 1994, because of the sick logic that said that they were. The Hutu women and children, the old and young, who comprised the majority in the camps in then-Zaïre between 1994 and 1996, were also the majority that died in the forests of Kivu in 1996 at the hands of the RPF and its allies. They died because of a similar logic: they were all *génocidaires* so they deserved to die. Those who have survived the camps and returned to Rwanda have been excluded from the political process as a group, again because they are potentially *génocidaires*.

It is not just the cycle of impunity that needs to be broken in Rwanda, but the logic that justifies or excuses the exclusion and death of thousands of people on the basis of ethnic labels. As Catherine Newbury has pointed out, the development and entrenchment of the "corporate perception of ethnicity" in Rwanda is one of the most troubling outcomes of the genocide (C. Newbury 1998:7). This spiral of blame and self-justification continues a well-entrenched pattern of power in Rwanda (C. Newbury 1998:7–24). This pattern also persists in the tendency to characterize only one group as the victims of genocide, and to deny the existence of any other victims. This spiral of blame and self-justification has also taken a cruel twist in Burundi. Here the Tutsi elites have taken the deplorable killings of Tutsi that followed the assassination of the Burundian president in October 1993[10] and turned them into a history of the persecution of the Burundian Tutsi. This strategy was also used in 1973 in Burundi when the Tutsi-dominated government, in a white paper to the UN, characterized the slaughter of Hutu intellectuals—between 150,000 and 250,000 Hutu were killed and 100,000 fled the country—in which between 2,000 and 3,000 Tutsi were killed in reprisals, as a genocide against the Tutsi (Malkki 1995:35, 248). The white paper goes on to state that "only the guilty were punished" (Government of Burundi, 1972:9–11 cited in Malkki 1995:249). The same justification was used by the Rwandan Hutu extremists in 1994 and was also the reason given for the massacres in the camp for the internally displaced in Kibeho by the Tutsi-dominated RPF in 1995. For the Burundian Tutsi elites, this mantle of victim-hood provides the justification for the repression of the Burundian Hutu population, the exclusion of the Hutu from all spheres of public life, the stalling of peace negotiations, and the denial of the ongoing slaughter of the Burundian Hutu. In Rwanda, the RPF have used the excuse that all Hutu are potentially *génocidaires* to do much the same thing. For the RPF, the excuse that they were aiding the militias or bystanders explains away the death of civilians in the fighting between the RPF and the militias. It also explains the purges of the independent Hutu within the RPF government, such as Twagiramungu, Sendashonga, and Kanyarengwe, who criticized these rationales (Human Rights Watch 1999a:732–734; Prunier 1997:1–2; Sibomana 1999:163). Not only has the RPF continued the pattern of ethnic labeling but it has also shown the same intolerance for opposition as the previous regimes.

Sadly, the RPF regime has also done little to end corruption or to open up the government to democracy. Rather it has reproduced the pattern of clientalism, political exclusion, double language, and corruption of the previous regimes, acting with the same brutal disregard for the needs of the majority of the population as the previous regimes. The military controls the budget and forms a shadow government with power down to the lowest level. The Hutu in the cabinet are treated as figureheads who are purged out of the government with accusations of corruption if they show signs of independence or, more recently, are denounced as *génocidaires,* four or five years after the fact. This is worrying not only because of the impact it has on any future democracy,[11] but also because it echoes the strategies of the previous regime. The genocide was executed in Rwanda by a similar shadow government. When the officials and military at the top were unwilling to be party to the killings and to the organization of the genocide, their actions were often countermanded by subordinates who had more power in the transitional government than these superiors (Human Rights Watch/Africa 1999a). Although Pasteur Bizimungu, a Hutu, was the president of Rwanda in the early years of the regime, Paul Kagame, a Ugandan-raised Tutsi aristocrat and the strategist who won Rwanda for the RPF, along with the army he controls, has now expelled Bizimungu and become president.

The intolerance of opposition is not confined to those who criticize the government from within. There has been an intolerance to criticism from human rights advocates and the press. Journalists such as André Sibomana, who were persecuted under the Habyarimana regime, found themselves persona non grata under the current regime when they criticized its actions. One by one, many of the most vocal human rights activists have been forced to leave the country, have been killed, arrested, or have died of natural causes.[12] The press began to censor itself, as the regime became more repressive, and as more journalists were detained or killed. By 1999, the human rights organizations and the journalists still active in the country engaged in self-censorship to remain untouched. Some have chosen to act on behalf of the government (Sibomana 1999). Ironically, this is the tactic the Habyarimana regime adopted when it was required to allow an open opposition and a "free" press.

Clientalism and ethnic differentiation still control access to power and resources. The most powerful members of the current government are the "Ugandan" Rwandans who supported the RPF in the struggle for power. The Rwandan returnees who had been based in Burundi and in the Democratic Republic of Congo have been marginalized in the current regime. Nevertheless, the benefits and resources of the state have been reserved for these groups.[13] In comparison to the Tutsi and Hutu survivors of the genocide and the Hutu peasantry, these two groups are still much better placed. Tutsi survivors have been shunted off to "villagization" programs, ostensibly so that the government can better protect them, but in which they are not only vulnerable to *Interahamwe* reprisals but also to malnutrition and disease. Moderate Hutu, who are survivors, are ignored or accused of being collaborators (Human Rights Watch/Africa 1999a; Sibomana 1999; Wagner 1998). The urban areas are dominated by an expatriate Tutsi community that has little connection with the peasantry and fears them as potential *génocidaires* (Prunier 1997). One of the critical problems that the Habyarimana regime faced was the growing fissure between its rural population (over 90 percent) and its urban-based elites (Uvin 1998). The new government has continued this pattern with a new ethnic overlay (Prunier 1997). The old urban Hutu who have returned have melted into the countryside, because those who have dared to reclaim their businesses and houses in the urban centers have been denounced and sent to prison. The new Tutsi urban elite has taken over these properties and remains indifferent to the needs of the peasantry (Prunier 1997). The Hutu peasantry, who were internally displaced or refugees, have returned under a cloud, tolerated only if they remain docile. In the northwest, where the militias are still active, they have been herded into "villages" that are inadequately serviced and protected. Despite considerable evidence that these types of "villagization" programs have never worked, whether for protection, the provision of services, or access to innovation, *and* have often driven the peasantry into the arms of the opposition, the RPF government is bent on pursuing it.

Overall, little has changed in Rwanda. Every Rwandan government since Rwabugiri took power in the 1860s has followed the same pattern of power: each has centralized power and resources into the hands of a tiny fraction of the elite, each has not tolerated opposition, and each has faced a violent and disputed succession, with a "winner takes all" approach to rule. The end result is a society with increasing inequality, and one in which access to power and resources continues to be based on ethnic and regional politics and personal clientage. At the grassroots level, these factors underpin the most striking feature of the Rwandan enterprises: the relationship between clientalism and access to the means of production and markets. These patterns of power have also created the household relations that condition the organization of labor: the nature of piecework, the lack of family labor in both big and small industries, and the role of women's labor in agriculture in reproducing labor in industry. These patterns of power created the exclusionary politics of the colonial period and the two Hutu-dominated postcolonial regimes. They also led to the genocide. Finally and tragically, these patterns of power also underpin the actions of the current regime.

Appendix A
Various Chronologies for the Rwandan Kings

	Approximate Dates of Reign According to		
King	Vansina	Rennie	D. Newbury
¹Ndahiro Ruyange	?–1386*	1424–1451*	
²Ndoba	1386–1410*	1451–1447*	
³Samembe	1410–1434*	1447–1505*	
⁴Nsoro Samukondo	1434–1458*	1505–1532	Newbury list
⁵Ruganzu Bimbwa	1458–1482*	1532–1559*	begins here
⁶Cylima Rugwe	1482–1506*	1559–1586	
⁷Kigeri Mukobanya	1506–1528*	1586–1588	
⁸Mibambwe Mutabazi	1528–1552*	1588–1593*	
⁹Yuhi Gahima	1552–1576*	1593–1603*	
¹⁰Ndahiro Cyamatare	1576–1600*	1603–?*	
¹¹Ruganzu Ndoori	1600–1624*	1603–1630*	near or after 1700
¹²Mutara Semugeshi	1624–1648*	1630–1657*	
¹³Kigeri Nyamushera	1648–1672*	1657–1684*	
¹⁴Mimbabwe Gisanura	1672–1696*	1684–1711*	
¹⁵Yuhi Mazimpaka	1696–1720*	1711–1738	
¹⁶Karemeera Rwaka	1720–1744*	1738–1756*	
¹⁷Cylima Rujugira	1744–1768*	1756–1765*	more reliable
¹⁸Kigeri Ndabarasa	1768–1792*	1765–1792*	evidence for
¹⁹Mibambwe Sentabyo	1792–1797*	1792–1797*	these kings
²⁰Yuhi Gahindiro	1797–1830*	1797–1830*	
²¹Mutara Rwogera	1830–1860*	1830–1860	
²²Kigeri Rwabugiri	1860–1895	1860–1895	
²³Mibambwe Rutarindwa	1896	1895–1896	
²⁴Yuhi Musinga	1896–1931	1896–1931	
²⁵Mutara Rudahigwa	1931–1959	1931–1959	

*estimated

Sources: D. Newbury (1994); Rennie (1972); Vansina (1962).

Note: David Newbury argues that many of the kings and dates noted before the Mwami Cylima Rujugira are at odds with chronologies from neighboring kingdoms' oral histories. He contends that many of these latter chronologies have been altered in order to conform to the chronology proposed by the Abbé Kagame. D. Newbury indicates that there is "very little evidence to assert the historicity of the kings in the cycle between Ruganzu and Rujugira" (D. Newbury 1994:210).

I have marked these disputed kings in italics and noted D. Newbury's concerns in the appropriate places.

Appendix B
European Contact and the German Colonial Period

1878 Henry Morton Stanley visits Lake Ihema in the southeast of Rwanda.

1884 Rwanda defined as German territory in the Congolese-German Agreement; however, no move was made to annex Rwanda.

1892 Oscar Baumann finds the source of the Kagera River in the south of Rwanda.

1894 Count von Götzen introduced at the court to Rwabugiri.

1895 Rwandan forces encounter Belgian troops at Shangi. The Rwandans are slaughtered. The Germans notify the Belgians that they are in violation of the Congolese-German Agreement. Belgians leave.

1897 Hauptman Ramsay ordered by Germans to open Rwanda to trade. He visits the court with three hundred soldiers.

1898 The German post at Shangi established.

1899 German military creates the "military region" of Ruanda-Urundi in Usumbura (now Bujambura). The king *(mwami)* agrees to German protection. Rwanda established as a tributary of Germany without being obliged to pay tribute by the Germans.

1907 De Kandt installed as Resident in Rwanda, creating an administrative post in Kigali. There is an increase in German exactions on the populace.

1914 August 15—World War I begins in Rwanda.

1916 Belgians penetrate Rwanda, taking the German administrative post and the royal capital, Nyanza, within a few days of each other.

Sources: Des Forges (1972); Nahimana (1987).

Appendix C
The Belgian Colonial Period

1916 Belgians penetrate Rwanda, taking the German administrative post and the Royal capital, Nyanza within a few days of each other.

1917 Official Belgian colonial rule established. Head tax introduced. Belgian "reforms" of *uburetwa* (cattle clientage) and chiefs' powers. Shift toward support of Tutsi rule.

1920s Obligatory cultivation and *akazi* (corvée for public works) introduced.

1925 Nyanza school reserved for Tutsi only.

1926 Belgian administrative reforms began. Abolition of cattle and war chiefs, and reduction of remaining chiefs. Land prestations modified.

1926–1930 Hutu chiefs replaced by Tutsi.

1928 Guidelines for all mission schooling that discriminated against Hutu and favored Tutsi.

1931 King Musinga deposed by the Belgians; Rudahigwa enthroned November 16.

1931–1933 Money payments substituted for land prestations.

1931 Program for coffee cultivation introduced.

1934 Money payment for all prestations given in kind.

1939 Money payment for *uburetwa* (land clientage in which agriculturalists who received land from a chief owed labor service to the chief, a low status form of clientage) allowed for some categories of people (i.e., contract laborers).

1949 *Uburetwa* replaced by tax.

1954 *Ubuhake* (cattle clientage in which the relationship was marked by the transfer of the usufruct of a cow from the patron to the client, a high status form of clientage) abolished.

1959 King Rudahigwa dies in July. King Ndahindurwa enthroned by conservative Tutsi factions.

1959 Hutu uprising started in November.

1960 Ndahindurwa deposed.

1961 Elections supervised by UN, in which Hutu parties won an overwhelming majority and the monarchy was rejected through a referendum.

1962 Independence from European rule.

Sources: Chrétien (1985); Des Forges (1969, 1972, 1986); Lemarchand (1977); C. Newbury (1988); Vidal (1973).

Appendix D
Prestations, *Corvées*, Taxes, and Obligations
(1898–1940)

I. Customary Prestations by 1898

- Seven kinds of tribute in kind *(ikoro)*, owed by the chiefs and subchiefs to the king, collected from the population.
- Customary cultivation *(butaka)* of the chief's land.
- Delivery of agricultural produce at harvesttime.
- Guarding the chief's hut at night.
- "Gifts" that traditionally accompanied the payment of tribute in kind.
- Construction and upkeep of the chiefs' compounds.

II. Colonial transformations

- *Uburetwa* labor in which each family was obliged to provide 2 days labor out of 5 (146 days a year)
- Prestations in kind turned into a money tax (1931).
- Money tax for all prestations in kind (1934).

I. Additional Colonial Obligations

1910s
- Introduction of head tax (1917) levied by the chiefs on behalf of the European administration, sharply increased the demands made upon the population.

1920s
- Introduction of *akazi*, "corvée labor," which added eleven days per adult male per year, for the construction of roads and upkeep, the construction of public buildings, drainage projects, anti-erosion projects, and reforestation.
- Obligatory crops (40 to 50 acres of manioc, sweet potatoes, buckwheat, etc).

1930s
- Intensification of obligatory crop cultivation, roadbuilding, and public projects.

Sources: Chrétien (1978); Lemarchand (1977).

Notes

CHAPTER 1

1. Gender refers to "socially constructed and historically variable relationships, cultural meanings and identities through which biological sex differences which become socially significant" (Laslett and Brenner 1989:382). Gender relations arise out of these identities and shape and constrain the actions of persons defined by those categories (Robertson and Berger 1986:23). The assumption that gender relations often place women in an unequal position is implicit in many definitions. Judith Lorber, for instance, argues that "as a social institution, gender is a process of creating distinguishable social statuses for the assignment of rights and responsibilities. As part of a stratification system that ranks these statuses unequally, gender is a major building block in the social structures built on these unequal statuses" (Lorber 1995:32). I would argue that unequal statuses that subordinate women can be an aspect of gender relations in particular situations, but the exact nature of gender relations is a question for analysis, not a given condition, even in stratified systems (Jefremovas 2000).

2. During the period of the Kayibanda and Habyarimana regimes, the end of colonialism and the fighting that followed was called the "Social Revolution."

3. Whether these were ethnic groups, castes, or classes has been a major debate in the literature on Rwanda and will be discussed in detail in chapter 4.

4. Most would have farmed some land and kept a small herd of livestock: some cattle, goats, and sheep.

5. There were regional concentrations, with the northwest region having the smallest proportion of Tutsi and the largest of Hutu, but there were no regions in which there were not members of all three ethnic groups.

6. Clientage, clientalism, and clientship have all been used to describe the workings of systems based on the relationship between the patron and client in many African societies (Lemarchand 1977:291–293, 297–298). George M. Foster argues that patron-client relations "tie people ... of significantly different socio-economic statuses, ... who exchange different kinds of goods and services (Foster 1967:216). In this book, the term *clientage* will be used to refer to the vertical links, both formal and informal, maintained between individuals in significantly different socioeconomic posi-

tions. The foundation on which these links are built can vary from society to society; however, it is interesting to note that kin ties *can* form the basis of patron-client ties. Karen Sacks argues that in Buganda the centralization of power in the hands of the king created a system where "kinship became a basis for establishing vertical, dyadic, clientage relations" (Sacks 1982:201). In Rwanda, kinship is one of a number of avenues for establishing patron-client relations. An analysis of the evolution of patron-ties and clientage from the precolonial period up to the present is essential for understanding contemporary Rwandan society.

7. The country is divided into *prefectures* that are in turn divided into *communes*, which are divided into *secteurs*, which are divided into a number of *cellules*.

8. In order to understand this density and its meaning for Rwandans, it is necessary to pull together figures from diverse sources and from different time periods.

9. These two areas responded to the genocide very differently. Gisenyi was the site of massacres of Tutsi from 1990 to 1993 and answered the calls for the genocide from the first days of April. Butare resisted the calls for massacres during the period leading up to the genocide and resisted the calls for the genocide for the first weeks, until the government brought in the military and militias to start the killing.

10. In the case of Gatovu, the political division coincides with a geographic division. Gatovu is a hill surrounded by marshland on three sides and a road on the fourth side.

11. Almost all of the interviews were conducted with the help of an assistant using semistructured surveys, usually at the work site or home of the informant. In addition to specific survey data and interviews on brick and tile production and marketing, material on household composition and household economic data was collected from each informant. These interviews focused on agriculture (production, labor, consumption, and marketing) and included questions on household and family composition (with questions on migration, occupation and work histories of family members). The data were collected over a twenty-four-month period. Information was also gathered and checked through open-ended key-informant interviews, group discussions, participant observation, and discussions with Rwandan and Western peers from February 1984 until August 1988.

12. Although the technique used to fire these tiles requires that some bricks are produced in each firing, most produced only enough bricks to create the base for the tiles.

13. With the help of two research assistants, I collected similar data on a total of 310 households for comparison. To analyze this data, I have broken down these 310 households into three categories: (1) households involved in brick and tile making; (2) households primarily involved in subsistence agriculture with some petty trade; and (3) households involved in other small industries, in salaried work, or in some form of wage labor outside of brick or tile production.

14. In Ngoma I interviewed almost all the small- and medium-size producers. At the time of the fieldwork there was also a very large undertaking that was manufacturing bricks for a development project under the direct supervision of the project itself.

15. In Huye, I worked only in one section of the marsh. Production in this marsh is very extensive and varied. In addition to the private industries involved in brick production, there was also a group of kilns being mounted and fired by prisoners for government use and there were a number of kilns producing bricks for a local mission.

16. I interviewed 15 from the largest enterprise, 9 from the second, 7 workers and the owner of the third, and 1 worker from the fourth. I also interviewed 4 members of the cooperative, 1 of whom was working for the largest entrepreneur and 2 of whom had worked as laborers in other enterprises.

17. These workers made it clear that they sold staple crops even though they also had to buy staples to feed their families. This did not happen among the workers in the south, who sold only surplus.

CHAPTER 2

1. See Scott Cook (1984), James Keddie and William Cleghorn (1980), and UNIDO (1969, 1971) as a basis of comparison.

2. Catherine Newbury discusses two such industries in western Rwanda that operated in the 1940s, employing 1,150 workers between them (C. Newbury 1988:175–176).

3. There was also one large capacity, multichambered semicontinuous kiln, know in Rwanda as the "Chinese" kiln, and one large industrial continuous kiln in Kigali. These were so uncommon that they will not be discussed here.

4. The exchange rate between 1983 and 1988 was relatively stable at 100 FRw to 1USD.

5. Agricultural laborers earned 100 FRw per day in the south and 80 FRw per day in the north in 1983–1988.

6. The largest entrepreneur in my survey had investigated its possibilities. She concluded that it was not worth the investment because it would take ten years to pay off, it would require an ongoing investment in upkeep and specialized personnel, and it would not suit the scale of her enterprise (she fires 1.5 million bricks a year), especially given that brick prices had virtually halved between 1980 and 1985 (from 5 FRw to 3 FRw).

7. A tile or brick that is laid out to dry or, as one informant put it, "a tile that has its true form, that is completed, smooth, pretty and ready to fire."

8. The capacity to hire wage labor, per se, did not make these enterprises more competitive.

9. Five FRw a tile and 3 FRw per brick were the going rate; however intense competition frequently led to lowering of these prices.

10. Despite this I saw much smaller clamp kilns in marshes near Bukavu in the Democratic Republic of Congo (then Zaïre).

CHAPTER 3

1. This coupled with the extraction of surplus value by nonproducers defines capitalist enterprises according to Michael Burawoy (1985:32).

2. Stoking the kiln is a skilled job in other countries (Cook 1984:94). In Rwanda it was not considered a highly skilled job. Stokers were called *zamus* (watchmen), a job category that is normally despised and poorly paid.

3. Rent for these sorts of houses ran from $600 (60,000 FRw) for a very small house to $1,000 (100,000 FRw) per month. The average functionary's salary ran from $100 to $150 per month, and a soldier's salary would have been considerably less.

4. These boys, between the ages of 10 and 13, came to the marsh looking for wage labor. They earned up to 100 FRw a day, usually buying cigarettes, beer, and occasionally clothing with their earnings. These boys were no longer in school. They worked as casual labor when they could find work.

5. This is the equivalent of a Grade 8 education and means that she had two years of training in domestic arts, that is, cooking, sewing, embroidery, knitting, and child care.

6. However, providing an advance was a minimal risk, because, it was not worth the employee's time to leave without fulfilling his obligations. He could be taken to court where he would be likely to lose to his more powerful and influential employer and to face a stiff fine or the potential confiscation of his property.

7. At the time of the interviews, Uganda was very politically and economically unstable while the economy of Rwanda was thriving.

8. Because the clay was dug dry and the water was drawn from a spring across the highway, the yards in Gisa had a different system. In this site, the owners hired men to draw water and to prepare the clay. However, the vast majority of enterprises worked in the marshes where clay preparation was less arduous.

9. Gisa and Pfunda are situated in the rich black soil belt of the north. The red soil land in Butare is markedly poorer in quality. The poorest soils are found in the Nil-Zaire crest, on which are found Cyangugu, Gikongoro, and Kibuye *prefectures*.

10. In all the marshes in this study dominated by small producers there was only one producer, Vestine, who hired labor and never worked in the production process. Her case will be discussed in chapter 6 because of the impact of gender on her capacity to mount an enterprise.

11. The fourth entrepreneur, whose business was defunct at the time of the interviews, was run by a young woman named Vestine. This case is discussed in chapter 6 because gender relations played a major role in the loss of her enterprise.

12. One of the means by which pieceworkers try to cut down on the time needed to produce tiles is by watering down the clay and doing minimal cleaning and kneading. This problem is discussed in various books on brick and tile making in the Third World. It is clear that "The better and more uniform the quality of the product

required the greater must be the control exercised ... over the various stages of the clay preparation. It is possible to make indifferent ware from adequately prepared clay; it is not possible to make good ware from inadequately prepared clay" (UNIDO 1969:42). What makes adequately prepared clay is also clear:

> Clay that still contains stones, pebbles, lumps, roots etc., or varies significantly in its plasticity on its arrival at the forming stage will certainly make inferior bricks, and may well interfere with the running of the forming machines. Human moulders are obviously more discriminating than forming machines in this respect, but their productivity still suffers to some extent if they have constantly to interrupt their moulding rhythm to accommodate variations in clay plasticity. (Keddie and Cleghorn 1980:16)

However, the authors continue: "But there is a reported tendency of human clay preparers, to ease their task by adding water to soften the clay to the point where it no longer holds its shape properly after moulding" (Keddie and Cleghorn 1980:16). Preparation of the clay by the owner is one way to insure both quality and speed. This explains why several of the richer producers preferred to do this less-skilled task themselves.

13. This cooperative and its problems strongly resembled the one discussed by Johan Pottier. In this cooperative, too, there was little cooperation, and the elites tried to maintain control over the labor force without redistributing funds or repaying debts. Pottier states that the general membership of the multifunctional cooperative he analyzed felt that committee members had "'long stomachs' that craved cash. Eating cash [was] common amongst committee members" (Pottier 1989a:57). Much the same could be said of the cooperative in Gatovu.

14. Six out of seven members in this cooperative were kin. They all volunteered the names of kin who made tiles, but none of them mentioned the relationship in the description of the organization of the cooperative. Without my direct questions on relatives who worked in brick or tile making there would have been no mention of the fact at all. Moreover, two of the sons of members of the Pfunda cooperative, Leopold and Pascal, did not work with their fathers, both stating that they preferred to work elsewhere.

15. There are three women entrepreneurs who run capitalist enterprises. Their cases are discussed in chapter 6.

CHAPTER 4

1. David Newbury's 1997 discussion of Rwandan attempts to claim parts of Kivu, Zaïre (now the Democratic Republic of Congo) on historical grounds illustrates this process superbly.

2. Other pastoral groups who have been classified as Nilotic, such as the Maasai, who live with those who speak "Bantu" languages, speak a separate language. There is no evidence that this was ever the case for the Rwandan and Burundian Tutsi.

3. The chronology and even the existence of various kings in the early period before Cylilima Rujugira is very shaky and before the eighteenth century the list of kings is unreliable. See D. Newbury (1994) for an in-depth discussion of the problems associated with the accepted chronologies and a list of kings of Rwanda. Because of this, I have chosen not to attribute dates to this period and to note that the events attributed to specific kings may have been a case of the "telescop[ing] of complex processes . . . attributing the introduction of complex phenomena to a single moment in time by a single process" that D. Newbury argues can be a feature of oral sources (D. Newbury 1994:207).

4. The dates and feats attributed to Rwabugiri have a somewhat firmer basis because they are much more recent and have some corroborating data from neighboring chronologies and oral histories.

5. René Lemarchand argues that in Burundi, the term *Hutu* meant "servant" or "social son" (Lemarchand 1994a:20).

6. This was an inherited position, the heir being chosen by the previous lineage head.

7. This intermarriage did not constitute a block to promotion, as many of these people gained prominent positions.

8. The extent to which land was considered to be privately owned was reflected in the nature of the crops that are grown on it. The planting of bananas, coffee, and trees symbolized permanent occupation and comprised a claim on the land.

9. However, this is not as straightforward as it seems. Women's control over land was lost upon marriage, when rights were transferred to the husband.

10. Over time, this rule was rarely respected.

11. The upper slope and hilltop lands are predominantly individually held lineage lands or privately held lands. Land on the lower slopes was acquired through the *commune*, and was almost invariably handed out on a patronage basis. This land could be sold with the permission of the *commune*, it could be rented out by the owner, and could lie fallow for a long period of time before the *commune* reappropriates it (Meschy 1973:76–77). In this way it strongly resembled the individually held land just discussed.

12. There is some evidence that occasionally rich Hutu, who gained favor with the court, married Tutsi women and their children became Tutsi, but this appears to have been uncommon by the turn of the century.

CHAPTER 5

1. I draw this term from Gavin A. Smith's discussion of small producers in Spain (Smith 1990).

2. In this discussion, the concept of the reproduction of labor is used in the Marxist sense as "the renewal from one round of production to another of the social

and technical elements of production and of the relations among them" (Friedmann 1980:162). Olivia Harris and Kate Young point out that the concept of reproduction encompasses three separate meanings, located at "different levels of abstraction and generality" (Harris and Young 1981:113). Therefore, "it is necessary to distinguish social reproduction of a particular social formation, from the reproduction of labor itself; and further to distinguish the latter from the specific forms of biological reproduction" (Harris and Young 1981:113). The particular focus of the following discussion is on "the reproduction of adequately socialized, adequately nourished labor" (Harris and Young 1981:123) on a day-to-day basis, although the activities discussed also clearly reproduce the whole system over time.

3. Married women's land is controlled by their husbands, although it does not belong to the man's patrilineage. Widows can distribute the land they have brought into the marriage, but once it is inherited it belongs to their sons and is passed on patrilineally.

4. One sheltered a neighboring woman and her children, the other a sister and her children. These two cases were temporary arrangements, especially the case of the neighbor. It was rare that a household would take in an unrelated woman, but she had fled the persecution of the first wife and expected to go home when her husband returned from a trip.

5. This has been described as the "house-property complex" by Max Gluckman (1971) and its implications for inheritance in a pan-African study are discussed by Jack Goody and Joan Buckley (1973).

6. This market was established to the point where Claudine Vidal argues that a list of equivalents could easily be drawn up, for instance, one untanned cowhide = 30 kilos of beans = 1 young goat = 1 hoe (Vidal 1974:68).

7. There were two men in my survey who were landless. Both rented land on which they grew staples.

8. See also Bonaventure Habimana (1973:752–753), Helen Codere (1973: 246–247), Ethel M. Albert (1971:179–215), and HRDD (1975:47–70, esp. 48–49).

9. National law, at that time, did not allow coffee to be intercropped. This policy was enforced and caused considerable resentment among the peasantry.

10. This situation mirrors the one discussed by F. Mackenzie (1995), but, unlike the case she discusses, women in Rwanda could not withdraw labor from their husbands' cash crops. Discussing a similar situation in Tanzania, Susan Rogers characterizes this type of system as "a gender system in which men control the lives of wives and children but are not economically responsible for them" (Rogers 1982:34).

11. A local women's group recommended that projects meant to increase women's cash-earning possibilities concentrate on projects that bring in small sums of money over time, rather than those that generate large sums all at once, so that women can retain control over their income.

12. The vast majority of bananas grown in Rwanda are varieties destined for beer making; however about 10 percent are food varieties (Jones and Egli 1984).

13. Some households never saw these "staples." Cooking oil in particular was a luxury in the poorest neighborhoods.

14. Ostensibly, it was the same as the south: 0.5 FRw per brick.

15. In the northwest, the rainy seasons are longer with much heavier rainfalls, and there is always some rainfall throughout the dry seasons.

CHAPTER 6

1. Claire Robertson and Iris Berger define critical resources broadly: "Resources . . . may include jobs, wages, land, labor power, cattle, as well as education or skills" (Robertson and Berger 1986:14).

2. I know of a number of cases where this has happened. Widows also had a very precarious hold on their husband's property in much of Uganda. The husband's kin could seize all property, whether it was brought into the marriage by the husband or wife, and expel her from her home (Obbo 1980:13, 34).

3. It was often pointed out in Rwanda, that in former times women who became pregnant before marriage were killed (Codere 1973:144). It is not clear how often this really happened, but the threat provided a powerful sanction against premarital pregnancy. Certainly, people discussing the rising rate of illegitimate births, harkened back to the "good old days."

4. Christine Obbo makes the same argument for Uganda (Obbo 1980:153, 156).

5. Obbo argues that in Uganda polygyny gives wives greater freedom because "a man can't control them all" (Obbo 1980:39). Vestine's father clearly allowed his wife to manage her resources as she saw fit. It would appear that in this case, polygyny gave his wife considerable freedom.

6. Females should always remain well covered. Even tiny baby girls must have their genitals covered. Women tell very small children, "Cover yourself or the men will see your genitals. How shameful!"

7. I met them through different people in different locations for my initial interviews. At the time I first met Christophe I had only heard of a "remarkable woman who ran her own brickyard"; I had not yet met her. Women do not take their husbands' surnames at marriage as Rwandan surnames are actually "given" names. Each person in every family has a different name.

8. In this region of Rwanda, most of the tea is cultivated on government plantations. Devota appears to have had a holding on the periphery of one of these.

9. In all my interviews, I had only one other such case. In this other case, the husband managed the land for his wife's family and his sons inherited this land as they married. None of Devota's sons was married at the time of the interviews.

10. *Les bandits* were reputed to be everywhere in Rwanda. There were whole areas where people were afraid to go because of them. Robbery is common and often bru-

tal. However, "bandits" also appear to make a habit of sitting outside weaker people's homes and terrorizing them with whispering campaigns.

11. The personal nature of these links is also illustrated by Helen Codere, in her life history of "Mukandori." Mukandori's story exemplifies the power woman could exercise, and the ways in which this power was linked to different men. Although Mukandori was frequently outspoken about changes in her rights and privileges under the colonial regime and after independence, she does not appear to find it remarkable that her fortunes were tied to her father, her husbands, lovers, and sons (Codere 1973:147–160).

12. African Rights (1995) documents the role that some elite women played in the genocide, but does not take this particular case of ethnic rivalry into account.

CHAPTER 7

1. Numbering of the dead in the genocide has been a source of an intense political struggle. Numbers from 50,000 to 1.5 million have been bandied about by various factions, depending on the political point that the proponents have wished to make. The most commonly accepted figure of 800,000 dead was set by Gérard Prunier (Prunier 1995:263). However, more recently, Human Rights Watch, has argued that this figure is more likely the number who died of all causes, not only in the genocide. They argue that the number killed in the genocide is closer to 507,000, and that the number killed by the Rwandan Patriotic Front (RPF) totals between 25,000 and 50,000 from April to August 1994 (Human Rights Watch 1999a:15–16). I have chosen to use the Human Rights Watch figures, because these figures have been compiled on the basis of more recent information and more precise data. Prunier's figures work on an estimate of the number of Tutsi presumed to live in Rwanda before the genocide and on estimates of survivors (Prunier 1995:263).

2. Although many authors, such as Catherine Newbury and David Newbury, have commented on this process, Peter Uvin (1998) provides detailed figures of both the structure of the Rwandan economy and of the crisis that the government faced in the late 1980s.

3. This is very misleading. Most Tutsi were commoners who were ruled. They were not rulers.

4. Until 1990, the regime of Habyarimana did not use overt ethnic violence as a political tool. However, after the invasion of the RPF in 1990 this changed. There was a systematic use of ethnic violence between 1990 and 1993, which was escalated in April 1994 (Human Rights Watch/Africa 1994; Reyntjens 1994:183–192). As in 1973, this process has been linked with the consolidation of power by a small elite and with regional politics (Reyntjens 1994:27–29).

5. This region, however, was the site of mob violence in the 1963 killings of Tutsi, where an estimated 5,000 out of the 10,000 estimated countrywide Tutsi deaths occurred.

6. The authors of the Human Rights Watch/Africa (1999a) book point out that this was not universal; different *communes* and *secteurs* responded differently, some responding to the call for killing before others (Human Rights Watch/Africa 1999a:432–494).

7. Discussing the events of the first three days with a number of Tutsi and Hutu who escaped from Kigali, it is striking how often both were threatened. As one man put it, "there was many a Hutu elite man on his knees in front of his Hutu gardener pleading for his life." This same man ran into the chauffeur from his department who told him proudly, "I'm rich now, boss, I've looted lots of houses!" Another Hutu family speaks of cowering in an interior corridor for three days because the mobs were running through the neighborhood. They left after the first three days because they decided that they "would rather die in the streets than like rats in the house."

8. See Johan Pottier (1995) for an in-depth discussion.

9. Needless to say, there are such cases, but this has become a blanket dismissal.

10. These killings were indiscriminate and unjustified, but many more Hutu than Tutsi died, most likely at the hands of the military. Although the government has begun to prosecute Hutu who have killed Tutsi, the government has not prosecuted anyone for the killing of Hutu after October 1993, nor have they prosecuted any of the military officers who were responsible for President Ndadaye's assassination (Human Rights Watch 1999b).

11. It should not be forgotten that this government took power by military force and not by democratic vote. Despite supposed local level elections that mimicked the showcase elections of the Habyarimana regime, it has shown no more interest in real democracy than any of the previous governments.

12. For example, Bishop André Sibomana was refused the right to leave the country for treatment of a rare health condition until it was too late to save him (Sibomana 1999).

13. In a 1995 proposal to the World Bank, the current regime proposed spending $30,000 per house for building housing for the *59ers* (the term used for the old refugee population to distinguish it from the refugees created by the 1990–1994 war many of whom returned in 1996). Although it sounds minimal to a Western ear, the average cost of a four-room brick-faced house with a tile roof, running water, and a toilet was less than $5,000 in 1988.

Bibliography

African Rights. 1994. *Rwanda: Death, Despair and Defiance.* London: African Rights.

———. 1995. *Rwanda Not So Innocent: When Women Become Killers.* London: African Rights.

Albert, Ethel M. 1971. "Women of Burundi: A Study of Social Values," *in* D. Paulme (ed.) *Women of Tropical Africa.* Berkeley and Los Angeles: University of California Press. pp. 179–215.

Barnett, Michael N. 1997. "The UN Security Council, Indifference, and the Genocide in Rwanda," *Cultural Anthropology* 12(4):551–578.

Battistini, Réne and Christian Prioul, 1981. "Problèmes Morphologiques du Rwanda," *in* CEGET (Centre d'études de Géographie Tropicale). *Les Milieux Tropicaux d'Altitude. Recherches Sur les Hautes Terres d'Afrique Centrale.* Talence: CEGET (CNRS), no. 42. pp. 9–31.

Brass, Tom. 1986. "The Elementary Strictures of Kinship: Unfree Relations and the Production of Commodities," *Social Analysis* 20: 56–68.

Burawoy, Michael. 1985. *The Politics of Production.* London: Verso.

Carney, Judith A. and Michael Watts. 1990. "Manufacturing Dissent: Work, Gender and the Politics of Meaning in a Peasant Society," *Africa* 60(2):207–240.

Chossudovsky, Michel. 1995a. *IMF-World Bank Mission Policies and the Rwandan Holocaust.* Third World Network Features. Third World Network. 228 Macalsiter Rd. 10400, Penang, Malaysia. E-mail article. 1287/95.

———. 1995b. *Rwandan Tragedy Not Just Due to Tribal Enmity.* Third World Network Features. Third World Network. 228 Macalsiter Rd. 10400, Penang, Malaysia. E-mail article. 1288/95.

———. 1997. *The Globalization of Poverty.* Penang, Malaysia: Third World Network.

Chrétien, Jean-Pierre. 1978. "Des Sédentaires Devenus Migrants: Les Motifs des Départs des Barundi et des Banyarwanda vers l'Uganda (1920–1960)," *Cultures et Développement* 10(1):71–101.

———. 1985. "Hutu et Tutsi au Rwanda et au Burundi," *in* Jean-Loup Amselle and Elikia M'Bokolo (eds.) *Au Coeur de L'Ethnie: Ethnies, Tribalisme et État en Afrique.* Paris: Éditions la découverte/Textes à l'appui. pp. 129–165.

———. 1992. "La Crise Politique Rwandaise," *Genève-Afrique* 30(2):121–140.

Chrétien, Jean-Pierre avec Reporters sans Frontières. 1995. *Rwanda: Les Médias du Génocides*. Paris: Kartala.

Codere, Helen. 1962. "Power in Rwanda," *Anthropologica* 4(1):45–85.

———. 1970. "Fieldwork in Rwanda, 1959–1960," *in* P. Golde (ed.) *Women In the Field: Anthropological Experiences*. Chicago: Aldine. pp. 141–164.

———. 1973. *The Biography of an African Society, Rwanda 1900–1960: Based on Forty-five Rwandan Autobiographies*. Tervuren, Belgium: Musée Royal de l'Afrique Centrale (Annales, Série in-8°, Sciences Humaines, no. 79).

Cook, Scott. 1984. *Peasant Capitalist Industry: Piecework and Enterprise in Southern Mexican Brickyards*. Latham, MD: University Press of America.

Cook, Scott and Leigh Binford. 1990. *Obliging Need: Rural Petty Industry in Mexican Capitalism*. Austin: University of Texas Press.

Crepeau, Pierre. 1985. *Parole et Sagesse: Valeurs Sociales dans les Proverbes du Rwanda*. Publication no. 29. Butare, Rwanda. Institut National de Recherche Scientifique.

Crepeau, Pierre and Simon Bizimana. 1979. *Proverbes du Rwanda*. Tervuren, Belgique: Musée Royal de l'Afrique Centrale (Annales, Série in-8°, Sciences Humaines, no. 97).

Davidson, Basil. 1992. *Black Man's Burden*. London: Currey.

Des Forges, Alison. 1969. "Kings without Crowns: The White Fathers in Ruanda," *in* Daniel F. McCall, Norman R. Bennett, and Jeffrey Butler (eds.) *Eastern African History*. Boston University Papers on Africa—3. New York: Praeger. pp. 176–207.

———. 1972. "Defeat Is the Only Bad News: Rwanda under Musiinga, 1896–1931," Ph.D. diss. Yale University.

———. 1986. "'The Drum is Greater than the Shout': The 1912 Rebellion in Northern Rwanda." David Crummey (ed.) *Banditry, Rebellion and Social Protest in Africa*. London: James Currey; Portsmouth, N.H.: Heinemann. pp. 311–331.

———. 1995. "The Ideology of Genocide," *Issue: A Journal of Opinion* 23(2):44–47.

Destexhe, Alain. 1994. *Rwanda: Essai sur le Génocide*. Bruxelles: Éditions Complexe.

Dorsey, Learthen. 1983. *The Rwandan Colonial Economy: 1916–1941*. Unpublished Ph.D. thesis. Michigan State University.

———. 1994. *Historical Dictionary of Rwanda*. Metuchen, N.J. and London: Scarecrow Press.

EIU (Economist Intelligence Unit). 1991. *Zaïre, Rwanda, Burundi: Country Profile 1990–1991. Annual Survey of Political and Economic Background*. London: Economist.

Fairhead, James. 1989. *"Paths of Authority:" Changing Food Security in a Village in Eastern Zaïre, as Roads Are Improved and the State "Rolls Back."* Presented at the United Nations Research Institute for Social Development (UNRISD) Seminar on Food Pricing and Marketing Reforms. Geneva, November 20–22.

———. 1990. "Fields of Struggle: Towards a Social History of Farming Knowledge and Practice in a Bwisha Community, Kivu, Zaïre." Ph.D. diss., School of Oriental and African Studies: University of London.

———. 1993. "Representing Knowledge: The 'New' Farmer in Research Fashions," *in* J. Pottier (ed.) *Practising Development: Social Science Perspectives.* London: Routledge. pp. 187–204.

Foster, George M. 1967. "The Dyadic Contract: A Model for the Social Structure of a Mexican Peasant Village," *in* Jack M. Potter, May N. Diaz, and George M. Foster (eds.) *Peasant Society: A Reader.* Boston: Little Brown. pp. 213–230.

Freedman, Jim. 1984. *Nyabingi: The Social History of an African Divinity.* Publication no. 26. Butare, Rwanda: Institut National de Recherche Scientifique.

Friedmann, Harriet. 1980. "Household Production and the National Economy: Concepts for the Analysis of Agrarian Formations," *Journal of Peasant Studies* 7 (2):158–184.

Gluckman, Max. 1971. "Marriage Payments and Social Structure amongst the Lozi and Zulu (postscript 1971)," *in* J. Goody (ed.) *Kinship: Selected Readings.* London: Penguin.

Godelier, Maurice. 1979. "The Appropriation of Nature (1)," *Critique of Anthropology* 13 and 14 (summer 1979).

Goody, Jack and Joan Buckley. 1973. "Inheritance and Women's Labour in Africa," *Africa* 43 (1973):108–121.

Gourevitch, Philip. 1998. *We Wish to Inform You that Tomorrow We Will Be Killed with Our Families: Stories from Rwanda.* New York: Farrar.

Gravel, Pierre B. 1965. "Life in the Manor in Gisaka (Rwanda)," *Journal of African History* 6: 323–331.

———. 1968a. *Remera: A Community in Eastern Ruanda.* The Hague: Mouton.

———. 1968b. "Diffuse Power as a Commodity: A Case Study from Gisaka (Eastern Rwanda)," *International Journal of Comparative Sociology* 9(3–4):163–176.

Gulati, Leela. 1982. "Jayamma, the Brick Worker," *in* Leela Gulati, *Profiles in Female Poverty: A Study of Five Poor Working Women In Kerala.* Oxford: Pergamon Press. pp. 35–62.

Gutekunst, Marc Daniel. 1995. "The Milles Collines and Kigali at War," *Issue: A Journal of Opinion* 23(2):12–17.

Guyer, Jane. 1981. "Household and Community in African Studies," *African Studies Review* 24(2/3):87–137.

Guyer, Jane and Pauline Peters. 1987. "Introduction: Conceptualizing the Household," *Development and Change* 18(2). Special Issue:179–213.

Habimana, Bonaventure. 1973. "La Condition Juridique, Politique et Social de la Femme au Rwanda," *Revue Juridique et Politique, Indépendence et Coopération* (Paris) 28:749–769.

Harris, Olivia. 1981. "Households as Natural Units," *in* K. Young, Carol Wolkowitz, and Roslyn McCullagh (eds.) *Of Marriage and the Market: Women's Subordination Internationally and its Lessons.* London: Routledge & Kegan Paul. 2d ed. 1984). pp. 49–68.

———. 1982. "Households and Their Boundaries," *History Workshop Journal,* Issue 13 (spring):143–152.

Harris, Olivia and Kate Young. 1981. "Engendered Structures: Some Problems in the Analysis of Reproduction," *in* J. S. Kahn and J. R. Llobera (eds.) *The Anthropology of Pre-Capitalist Societies.* London: Macmillan.

Hart, Gillian. 1992. "Imagined Unities: Construction of the 'Household' in Economic Theory," *in* S. Ortiz and S. Lees (eds.) *Understanding Economic Process.* Monographs in Economic Anthropology, no. 10. Lanham, Maryland: Academic Press of America. pp. 111–129.

Henn, Jeanne Koopman. 1988. "The Material Basis of Sexism," *in* Sharon B. Stichter and Jane Parpart (eds.) *Patriarchy and Class: African Women on the Home and Workplace.* Boulder and London: Westview.

HRDD (Human Resources Development Division—United Nations Economic Commission for Africa). 1975. "Women and National Development in African Countries: Some Profound Contradictions," *African Studies Review* 18:3:47–70.

Human Rights Watch/Africa. 1994. *Arming Rwanda: The Arms Trade and Human Rights Abuses in the Rwandan War.* Human Rights Watch/Africa Newsletter 6, 1.

Human Rights Watch. 1999a. *Leave None to Tell the Story: Genocide in Rwanda.* New York: Human Rights Watch; Paris: International Federation of Human Rights.

———. 1999b. "Burundi." *World Report.* Website: www.hrw.org.

IDRC (International Development Research Centre). 1989. "Bricks in Rwanda." Proposal to the Earth and Engineering Sciences Division. Manuscript.

Jackson, Cecile. 1993. "Women/Nature or Gender/History? A Critique of Ecofeminist Development," *Journal of Peasant Studies* 20(3):389–419.

Jefremovas, Villia. 1997. "Contested Identities: Power and the Fictions of Ethnicity, Ethnography and History in Rwanda," *Anthropologica* 39(1 and 2):91–104.

———. 2000. "Women Are Good with Money: The Impact of Cash Cropping on Class Relations and Gender Ideology amongst the Sagada Igorots of Northern Luzon, the Philippines," *in* Anita Spring (ed.) *Women Farmers and Commercial Ventures: Increasing Food Security in Developing Countries.* Boulder: Lynne Rienner. pp. 131–150.

Jones, Bruce. 1999a. "Civil War, the Peace Accords and Genocide in Rwanda," *in* Taisier M. Ali and Robert O. Matthews (eds.) *Civil Wars in Africa: Roots and Resolution.* Montreal and Kingston: MacGill-Queen's University Press. pp. 53–88.

———. 1999b. "The Arusha Peace Process," *in* Adelman, H. and Astri Suhrke (eds.) *The Path of a Genocide: The Rwanda Crisis from Uganda to Zaire.* New Brunswick, N.J. and London: Transaction Publishers. pp. 131–156.

Jones, William I. and Roberto Egli, 1984. *Farming Systems in Africa: The Great Lakes Highlands of Zaire, Rwanda and Burundi.* Washington, D.C.: World Band Technical Paper, no. 27.

Kagame, Alexis (l'abbé). 1972. *Une Abrégé de l'Ethno-histoire du Rwanda.* Butare: l'Université National du Rwanda (UNR).

Kamanzi, Callixte and Charles Rwanga. 1986. "Études de Cas: Briqueteries," *in* IDRC/CRDI et Ministere de l'Industrie des Mines et de l'Artisanat, *Atelier National De Recherche sur la Politique Technologique au Rwanda.* Kigali from 18 to 31 May.

Keddie, James and William Cleghorn. 1980. *Brick Manufacture in Developing Countries.* Edinburgh: Scottish Academic Press.

Kesby, John D. 1977. *The Cultural Regions of East Africa.* London, New York, and San Francisco: Academic Press.

Laslett, Barbara and Johanna Brenner. 1989. "Gender and Social Reproduction: Historical Perspectives," *Annual Review of Anthropology* 15:381–404.

Lem, Winnie. 1988. "Household Production and Reproduction in Languedoc: Social Relations of Petty Commodity Production in Merviel-lès-Béziers," *Journal of Peasant Studies* 15(4):500–529.

———. 1999. *Cultivating Dissent: Work, Identity and Praxis in Rural Languedoc.* Albany: State University of New York Press.

Lemarchand, René. 1970. *Rwanda and Burundi.* London: Pall Mall Press.

———. 1977. "Rwanda," *in* Rene Lemarchand (ed.) *African Kingships In Perspective.* London: Frank Cass & Co. pp. 67–92.

———. 1982. "The World Bank in Rwanda." African Studies Program: Indiana University. Mimeo.

———. 1994a. *Burundi: Ethnic Conflict and Genocide.* Cambridge, United Kingdom, New York, and Melbourne, Australia (with new preface 1996).

———. 1994b. "Managing Transition Anarchies: Rwanda, Burundi, and South Africa in Comparative Perspective," *Journal of Modern African Studies* 32(4):581–604.

———. 1998. "Genocide in the Great Lakes: Which Genocide? Whose Genocide?" *African Studies Review* 41(1):3–16.

———. 1999. *Ethnicity as Myth: The View from the Central Africa.* Paper: Center of African Studies: University of Copenhagen. May 4, 1999.

Longman, Timothy. 1995. "Genocide and Socio-political Change: Massacres in Two Rwandan Villages," *Issue: A Journal of Opinion* 23(2):18–21.

Lorber, Judith. 1995. *The Paradox of Gender.* New Haven: Yale University Press.

Lugan, Bernard. 1977. "Les Pôles Commerciaux du Lac Kivu à la Fin du XIXe Siècle," *Revue Française d'Histoire d'Outre-mer* 64(235):176–202.

———. 1981. "La Situation des Marchés Précoloniaux au Rwanda, Une Origine Politique ou Naturelle?" *in* CEGET (Centre d'études de Géographie Tropicale. *Les Milieux Tropicaux d'Altitude. Recherches sur les Hautes Terres d'Afrique Centrale.* Talence: CEGET (CNRS), no. 42. pp. 201–215.

Lugan, Bernard and Antoine Nyagahene. 1983. "Les Activités Commerciales du Sud Kivu au XIXe Siècle À Travers l'Exemple de Kinyaga (Rwanda)," *Cahiers d'Outremers* 36(141):19–48.

MacGaffey, Janet. 1988. "Evading Male Control: Women in the Second Economy in Zaïre," *in* Sharon B. Stichter and Jane L. Parpart (eds.) *Patriarchy and Class: African Women in the Home and Workplace.* Boulder: Westview.

Mackenzie, F. 1995. "'A Farm Is Like a Child Who Cannot Be Left Unguarded': Gender, Land, and Labour in Central Province, Kenya," *IDS Bulletin* 26(1):17–23.

Mair, L. 1961. "Clientship in East Africa," *Cahiers d'Études Africaines* 6(2):15–325.

Malkki, Liisa. 1995. *Purity and Exile: Violence, Memory, and National Cosmology among Hutu Refugees in Tanzania.* Chicago and London: University of Chicago Press.

Mamdani, Mahmood. 1996. "From Conquest to Consent as the Basis of State Formation: Reflections on Rwanda," *New Left Review* 216 (March/April):3–36.

Manson, Jack M. 1982. *Bricks in Alberta.* Edmonton, Canada: Co-op Press.

Maquet, Jacques J. 1961a. *The Premise of Inequality.* London: Oxford University Press.

———. 1961b. "Une Hypothèse pour l'Étude des Féodalités Africaines," *Cahiers d'Études Africaines* 6(2, 2):292–314.

———. 1967. "La Tenure des Terres dans l'État Rwanda Traditionnel," *Cahiers d'Études Africaines* 7(4, 28):624–636.

———. 1969. "Institutionalisation Féodale des Relations de Dépendance dans les Quatres Cultures Interlacustres," *Cahiers d'Études Africaines* 9(35):401–414.

Meschy, Lidia (misspelled in original: Meschi, Lydia). 1973. *Kanserege, Une Colline au Rwanda de l'Occupation Pionniere au Surpeuplement.* Thèse de doctorate de 3me cycle. Paris: École practique des hautes études (VIe section): CNRS.

———. 1974. "Évolution des Structures Foncières au Rwanda: Le Cas d'un Lignage Hutu," *Cahiers d'Études Africaines* 14(1, 53):39–51.

MINIPLAN. 1988. *Enquete Nationale sur le Budget et la Consommation (Milieu Rural).* Vols. 2–4. Kigali, Rwanda: Ministère du Plan.

Mujawamariya, Monique. 1994. *Rapport de Visite Effectuée au Rwanda du 1/9/94 au 22/9/94.* Montreal: Association Rwandaise pour la Défense des Droits de la Personne et des Libertés Publiques (ADL).

———. 1995. "Report of a Visit to Rwanda, September 1–22, 1994," *Issue: A Journal of Opinion* 23(2):32–38.

Nahimana, Ferdinand. 1987. *Le Blanc Est Arrivé, Le Roi Est Parti.* Kigali, Rwanda: Printer Set.

Newbury, Catherine. 1974. "Deux Lignages du Kinyaga," *Cahiers d'Études Africaines* 14(1, 53):26–38.

———. 1978. "Ethnicity in Rwanda: The Case of Kinyaga," *Africa* 48(1):17–29.

———. 1980. "*Ubureetwa* and *Thangata:* Catalysts to Present Political Consciousness in Rwanda and Malawi," *Canadian Journal of African Studies* 14(1):97–111.

———. 1983. "Colonialism, Ethnicity, and Rural Protest: Rwanda and Zanzibar in Comparative Perspective," *Comparative Politics* 15(3):253–280.

———. 1988. *The Cohesion of Oppression: Clientship and Ethnicity in Rwanda, 1860–1960.* New York: Colombia University Press.

———. 1992. "Rwanda: Recent Debates Over Governance and Rural Development," *in* G. Hyden and M. Bratton (eds.) *Governance and Politics in Africa.* Boulder: Lynne Rienner. pp. 193–210.

———. 1995. "Background to Genocide: Rwanda," *Issue: A Journal of Opinion* 23(2):12–17.

———. 1998. "Ethnicity and the Politics of History in Rwanda," Special Issue: Crisis in Central Africa, *Africa Today* 45(1):7–24.

Newbury, Catherine and David Newbury. 1994. "Rwanda: The Politics of Turmoil," *Africa Notes.* October: 1–2.

———. 1996. *Death and Demos: The Failure of Democratization in Rwanda.* Conference paper, "Transitions in Africa: Violence and the Politics of Participation," Niamey, Niger, June 4–7.

———. Forthcoming. "A Catholic Mass in Kigali: Contested Views of the Genocide and Ethnicity in Rwanda." *Canadian Journal of African Studies.*

Newbury, David. 1980a. "The Clans of Rwanda—A Historical Hypothesis," *Africa* 50(4):389–403.

———. 1980b. "Lake Kivu Regional Trade in the 19th century," *Journal des Africanistes* (Paris) 50(2):5–30.

———. 1981. "What Role Has Kingship? An Analysis of the *Umuganura* Ritual as Presented in Marcel D'Hertefelt and André Coupez (eds.) *La Royauté Sacrée de l'Ancien Rwanda* (1964)," *Africa-Tervuren* 27(4):89–101.

———. 1987. "'Bunyabungo:' The Western Rwandan Frontier, 1750–1850," *in* Igor Kopytoff (ed.) *The African Frontier: The Reproduction of Traditional African Societies.* Bloomington: Indiana University Press. pp. 162–192

———. 1994. "Trick Cyclists? Recontextualizing Rwandan Dynastic Chronology," *History in Africa* 21:191–217.

———. 1995a. "The Invention of Rwanda: The Alchemy of Ethnicity." Manuscript.

———. 1995b. "Rwanda: Genocide and After," *Issue: A Journal of Opinion* 23(2):4–7.

———. 1997. "Irredentist Rwanda: Ethnic and Territorial Frontiers in Central Africa," *Africa Today* 44(2):211–221.

———. 1999. "Ecology and the Politics of Genocide," *Cultural Survival* (winter), 2(4):32–35.

Obbo, Christine. 1980. *African Women: Their Struggle for Economic Independence*. London: Zed Press.

Olson, Jennifer M. 1994. *Factors Behind the Recent Tragedy in Rwanda*. Paper presented at "The Contribution of Key Factors in the Recent Tragedy in Rwanda: Poverty, Population and Environment," World Bank, Washington, D.C. November 2.

Parpart, Jane and Kathleen Staudt. 1989. "Women and the State in Africa," *in* Jane Parpart and Kathleen Staudt (eds.) *Women and the State in Africa*. Boulder and London: Lynne Rienner.

Pottier, Johan. 1989a. "Debating Styles in a Rwandan Cooperative: Reflections on Language, Policy and Gender," *in* Ralph Grillo (ed.) *Social Anthropology and the Politics of Language*. Sociological Review Monograph 36. London: Routledge.

———. 1989b. "'Three's a Crowd': Knowledge, Ignorance and Power in the Context of Urban Agriculture in Rwanda" *Africa* 59(4):462–477.

———. 1990. *Food Security in Rwanda: Beyond the Politics of Pricing and Marketing Reform*. Presented at the UNRISD Seminar on Food Pricing and Marketing Reforms. Geneva Nov. 20–22. Subsequently republished as: Pottier, Johan. 1993. "Taking Stock: Food Marketing Reform in Rwanda, 1982–1989," *African Affairs* 92:5–30.

———. 1995. "Representation of Ethnicity in Post-Genocide Writings on Rwanda," *in* Obi Igwara (ed.) *Ethnic Hatred and Genocide in Rwanda*. London: London School of Economics and Political Science, ASEN Publication. pp. 35–57.

Pottier, Johan and Augustin Nkundabashaka. 1989. *Intolerable Environments: Notes Towards a Cultural Reading of Agrarian Practice and Policy in Rwanda*. Presented at the EIDOS Workshop on Cultural Understandings of the Environment. London, June 22–24.

Pottier, Johan and John Wilding. 1994. *Food Security and Agricultural Rehabilitation in Postwar Rwanda, August–September 1994*. Report to Save the Children (SCF) United Kingdom. October.

Prioul, Christian. 1981. "Les Densités de Population au Rwanda," *in* CEGET (Centre d'études de Géographie Tropicale). *Les Milieux Tropicaux d'Altitude. Recherches sur les Hautes Terres d'Afrique Centrale*. Talence, France: CEGET (CNRS), no. 42. pp. 61–80.

Prunier, Gérard. 1993. "Éléments pour Une Histoire du Front Patriotique Rwandais," *Politique Africaine* 51 (October):121–138.

———. 1995. *The Rwanda Crisis: History of a Genocide*. New York: Columbia University Press.

———. 1997. *Rwanda: The Social, Political and Economic Situation in June 1997*. A Writenet Issue Paper. United Kingdom: Writenet (Internet publication).

Reader, J. 1999. *Africa: A Biography of the Continent*. New York: Alfred A. Knopf.

Rennie, J.K. 1972. "The Precolonial Kingdom of Rwanda: A Reinterpretation," *Transafrican Journal of History* 2:11–44.

Reyntjens, Filip. 1994. *L'Afrique des Grandes Lacs en Crise: Rwanda, Burundi 1988–1994*. Paris: Éditions Karthala.

Roberts, Penelope. 1988. "Rural Women's Access to Labour in West Africa," *in* Sharon B. Stichter and Jane L. Parpart (eds.) *Partiarchy and Class: African Women in the Home and Workplace*. Boulder: Westview.

Robertson, Claire and Iris Berger. 1986. "Introduction: Analyzing Class and Gender— African Perspectives," *in* Claire Robertson and Iris Berger (eds.) *Women and Class in Africa*. New York and London: Africana. pp. 3–24.

Rogers, Susan. 1982. "Efforts toward Women's Development in Tanzania: Gender Rhetoric vs. Gender Realities," *Women and Politics* 2(4):23–41.

Rwabukumba, Joseph and Vincent Mudandagizi. 1974. "Les Formes Historiques de la Dependance Personnelle dans l'Etat Rwandais," *Cahiers d'Études Africaines* 14(1, 53):6–25.

Sacks, Karen. 1982. *Sisters and Wives: The Past and Future of Sexual Equality*. Urbana: University of Illinois Press.

Sibomana, André. 1999. *Hope for Rwanda: Conversations with Laure Guilbert and Hervé Deguine*. London: Pluto Press.

Sider, Gerald. 1980. "The Ties that Bind: Culture and Agriculture, Property and Propriety in the Newfoundland Village Fishery," *Social History* 5(1):1–39.

Smith, Gavin A. 1990. "Negotiating Neighbours: Livelihood and Domestic Politics in Central Peru and the Pais Valenciano (Spain)," *in* Jane Collins and Martha Gimenez (eds.) *Work without Wages: Comparative Studies of Domestic Labor and Self-Employment*. Albany: State University of New York Press. pp. 50–69.

Stichter, Sharon B. and Jane L. Parpart. 1988. "Introduction: Towards a Materialist Perspective on African Women," *in* Sharon B. Stichter and Jane L. Parpart (eds.) *Patriarchy and Class: African Women in the Home and Workplace*. Boulder: Westview.

Toronto Star. October 6, 1984. "A Hint of Shangri-la Amid African Turmoil." Special report by Morris Ilyniak.

UNIDO (United Nations Industrial Development Organization). 1969. *The Establishment of the Brick and Tile Industry in Developing Countries*. New York: United Nations.

———. 1971. *Clay Building Materials Industries in Africa*. Report of the Workshop held in Tunis, December 6–12, 1970. New York: United Nations.

Uvin, Peter. 1998. *Aiding Violence: The Development Enterprise in Rwanda*. West Hartford, Conn.: Kumarian Press.

Vandersypen, Marijke. 1977. "Femmes libres de Kigali," *Cahiers d'Études Africaines* 17, 1, 65:95–120.

Vansina, Jan. 1962. *L'Evolution du Royaume Rwanda des Origines à 1900*. Brussels: ARSOM.

———. 1963. "Les Régimes Fonciers Ruanda et Kuba—Une Comparaison," *in* Daniel Biebuyck, (ed.) *African Agrarian Systems*. London: Oxford. pp. 348–363.

———. 1998. "The Politics of History and the Crisis in Central Africa," Special Issue: Crisis in Central Africa *Africa Today* 45(1):37–44.

Vidal, Claudine. 1969. "Le Rwanda des Anthropologues ou le Fétichisme de la Vache," *Cahiers d'Études Africaines* 9(3):384–401.

———. 1973. "Colonisation et Décolonisation du Rwanda: La Question Tutsi-Hutu," *Revue Française d'Études Politiques Africaines*. 91 July, 32–47.

———. 1974. "Économie de la Société Féodale Rwandaise," *Cahiers d'Études Africaines* 14, 1(53):52–74.

———. 1984. Enquétes sur l'Histoire et sur l'Au-dela: Rwanda, 1800–1970. *Homme* 24(3–4):61–82.

———. 1985. "Situations Ethniques au Rwanda," *in* Jean-Loup Amselle and Elikia M'Bokolo (eds.) *Au Coeur de l'Ethnie: Ethnies, Tribalisme et État en Afrique*. Paris: Éditions la découverte/Textes à l'appui. pp. 167–184.

———. 1991. *Sociologie des Passions (Cote d'Ivoire, Rwanda)*. Paris: Éditions Karthala.

Voss, Joachim. 1989. *An Anthropological Perspective on Agricultural Research*. Presented at the International Development Research Centre Seminar Series, Ottawa. Unpublished Manuscript.

———. 1992. "Conserving and Increasing On-Farm Genetic Diversity: Farmer Management of Varietal Bean Mixtures in Central Africa," *in* Joyce Lewinger Moock (ed.) *Diversity, Farmer Knowledge and Sustainability*. Geneva, N.Y.:Cornell University Press. pp. 34–51.

Wagner, Michele D. 1998. "All the Bourgmestre's Men: Making Sense of Genocide in Rwanda," Special Issue: Crisis in Central Africa, *Africa Today* 45(1):25–36.

Whitehead, Anne. 1984. "'I'm Hungry, Mum,'" *in* K. Young, C. Wolkowitz, and M. McCullagh (eds.) *Of Marriage and the Market*. London: CSE Books. pp. 89–111.

World Guide. 2001. "Rwanda," *The World Guide 2001/2002*. Oxford: New Internationalist Publications.

Yanagisako, Sylvia Junko. 1979. "Family and Household: The Analysis of Domestic Groups," *Annual Review of Anthropology* 8: 161–205.

Index

Agriculture: beer sales, 91–92, 93; cash crops, 4, 44, 70, 82, 86, 91*tab;* differing meaning of crops, 90; failure of, 89; meaning of sale of crops, 90; Northern, 44; obligatory, 68, 70, 74; seasonal, 57, 81; self-sufficiency and, 45; Southern, 44; subsistence, 4, 10, 18, 19, 85, 86; women in, 3, 86–88
Albert, Ethel, 65
Arusha Accords, 112
Assimilation, 2

Bagambiki, Emmanuel, 117
Barnett, Michael, 120
Battistini, Réne, 4
Baumann, Oscar, 129
Belgian Congo. *See* Democratic Republic of Congo
Belgium, 3, 66, 67–68
Berger, Iris, 98, 99, 135*n1*
Binford, Leigh, 29
Bizimana, Simon, 80
Boutros-Ghali, Boutros, 120
Brass, Tom, 83–85
Brick and roof tile industry. *See also* Bricks; Tiles; access to labor and, 81–83; adaptation to local conditions by, 1; capital needed, 24; in colonial period, 21; comparative, 29–30; cooperatives, 24; customers for, 42; domestic relations and, 83–86; economy of scale in, 30–31; employment rates, 21; family labor and, 18, 81–83; in Gisa, 40–42; growth of, 21–22; households and, 83–85; in Huye, 10, 12, 13*fig,* 37–40; labor intensity in, 29; labor organization, 2, 16, 19, 22, 35–57; labor process, 25–29, 31; land inheritance and, 81–83; larger-scale, 10; marriage and, 82; molds used, 27; in Ngoma, 10, 11*fig;* in the North, 40–42; owner involvement in, 35, 36–42; payment to workers in, 39, 40; in Pfunda, 12, 15, 16, 40–42; self-provisioning and, 90–94; skills needed, 24; in the South, 37–40; specialty bricks and, 24; techniques in, 21–31; technology and, 21–25

Bricks: capitalist organization for, 36, 138*n1;* capital needed, 24; drying, 27; economy of scale in, 30; formation, 27; forming, 36; going rate for, 137*n9;* hacking, 27; kilns, 21, 23*fig;* markets fir, 36; molds, 27, 42; refractory, 24; round-cornered, 42; specialty, 24, 42; underfiring, 22; unfired, 49; ventilated, 42
Brideprice, 88, 89
Bugesera: genocide in, 114
Burundi, 61, 65, 112, 113, 122, 123, 124, 125, 140*n5*
Butare, 6–7; clay digging in, 25; employment in, 21; genocide in, 114, 136*n9*

Carney, Judith, 83–85
Case studies: Devota, 105–106, 142*n9;* Emmanuel, 40–42; Gakuzi, 46, 82; Innocent, 50–51; Juvenal, 47–48, 82;

Case studies *(continued)*
  Mediatrice, 103–105; Northern entrepreneurs, 40–42; owner involvement, 37–42; ownership by married women, 103–105; production strategies, 45–51; Simon, 40–42; Southern entrepreneurs, 37–40; Telesphore, 40–42; Theodomir, 37–40; unmarried owner of business, 100–103; Vestine, 100–103, 138*n10,* 138*n11;* Vianney, 37–40; widow's business ownership, 105–106; women entrepreneurs, 100–106
Chossudovsky, Michel, 110
Chrétien, Jean-Pierre, 61, 68, 69, 71, 80, 134
Class: gender and, 19, 97–108; impact on everyday life, 97–108; relations, 2
Clay: access to, 36; digging patterns, 26; dry, 26; land, 35, 36, 51, 53; molding, 26–27; overburden, 25, 26; pits, 26; preparation for firing, 27, 32*tab;* preparing, 26–27; public lands, 7; selection, 29; weathering, 29; wet, 7, 26; winning, 25–26, 32*tab,* 36
Cleghorn, William, 24, 29
Clientage, 3, 125, 135*n6;* access to land and, 18, 35, 81; benefits of, 60; cattle, 71; in colonial period, 67, 68, 71–72; consolidation of, 64; development of, 81; hierarchy of, 64; inheritance and, 85; land, 71, 115; land access and, 30; land inheritance and, 81; lineages and, 63; political, 73–74; spread of, 65
Coalition pour le Défense de la République, 112
Codere, Helen, 72, 84, 87, 142*n3*
Colonial period, 66–76; agriculture in, 70; brick and roof tile industry in, 21; clientage in, 67, 68, 71–72; demands on labor in, 67; education in, 69; German era, 66–67, 129; labor relations in, 71–72; land tenure in, 71–72; out-migration during, 70; political reform in, 68; social relations in, 18; transformations during, 2
Congolese-German Agreement, 129
Cook, Scott, 29, 45, 138*n2*
Cooperation Suisse, 24
Cooperatives, 7, 16, 35, 51–55, 139*n13;* access to land and, 54, 55, 57; arbitrary creation of, 51; drawbacks of, 52, 53; equality of effort in, 54; financial difficulties in, 52; in Gatovu, 24, 51, 52; negligence in, 54; obligatory membership in, 51, 52; organizational issues in, 18, 52, 54
Corruption, 1, 72, 73, 110, 113
Crepeau, Pierre, 80
Culture, 3
Cyangugu: genocide in, 115, 117

Dallaire, Romeo, 120
Davidson, Basil, 60
Democracy: limited, 1, 111
Democratic Republic of Congo, 4, 79–81, 107, 125, 137*n10;* Belgian Congo, 70
Des Forges, Alison, 61, 64, 65, 67, 68, 69, 115
Development aid, 4
Divorce, 83, 88
Dorsey, Leathern, 87

Economic: autonomy, 99; relations, 2; restructuring, 73; structures, 73–74
Economy of scale, 16, 30–31, 36, 51, 82; alternative technologies and, 30
Education: access to, 2, 73, 74, 110; in colonial period, 69; low levels of, 85
Employment: nonfarm, 21; rural, 21
Ethnic: antagonisms, 61; differentiation, 125; exclusion, 2; fighting, 72; hatred, 114; violence, 19, 113, 143*n4*
Ethnicity, 2; access to resources and, 74; corporate perception of, 123; in determination of women's lives, 87; interpretations of, 59; origin of, 59; power and, 2; as source of tension, 61
Euro-assistance, 24

Fairhead, James, 75, 81, 87, 89, 90, 93
Family: brideprice and, 88, 89; claims on labor in, 93; control of children in, 81; divorce in, 83, 88; fragmentation of land holdings and, 79–81; income control in, 84; inequalities in, 3, 18, 56; inheritance and, 79–81, 84; labor, 3, 18, 56; lack of obligations in, 84; landlessness of some sons in, 79–81; limits of paternal power in, 81; marriage and, 83–85; polygyny and, 83, 84, 85, 99; self-provisioning and, 89–94
Freedman, James, 81
Fuel, kiln, 22, 24

Gahindiro, 63, 127*tab*
Gahinga-Muyaga Catholic Mission, 12
Gatovu, 6–7, 9*fig*; agricultural labor in, 92; clay digging in, 25, 26; cooperative kiln in, 24, 51, 52; festive labor in, 92; genocide in, 136*n10*; production strategies in, 45–51; sale of crops in, 90, 91*tab*
Gender: access to means of production and, 98; class and, 19, 97–108; defining, 135*n1*; impact on everyday life, 97–108; labor and, 3; relations, 2, 18, 87, 94–95, 135*n1*
Genocide: background issues, 109–113; circumstances leading to, 19; in the East, 115; ethnic propaganda and, 112, 113; fictions of tradition and, 114–115; logic of, 112; media and, 112, 113; in the North, 114–115; orchestration of, 119; political manipulation and, 118–121; preconditions for, 1–2; regional differences in, 113–118, 144*n6*; regional dynamics and, 118–121; relations, 19; responses to, 136*n9*; in the South, 118; in the Southwest, 115, 117; state sponsorship of, 113–118; systematic violence in, 118–121
Germany, 3, 65, 66–67, 129
Gikongoro, 4; genocide in, 114, 117

Gisa, 17*fig*; brick and roof tile industry in, 40–42; clay digging in, 26; genocide in, 114; owners in, 36; sale of crops in, 90, 91*tab*
Gisenyi, 12, 16, 40; employment in, 21
Gitarama, 4; genocide in, 114
Gourevitch, Philip, 122
Gravel, Pierre, 60, 65, 87

Habimana, Bonaventure, 84, 88, 90, 93
Habyarimana, Agathe, 114–115
Habyarimana, Juvenal, 1, 19, 73, 74, 109, 110, 111, 112, 113, 115, 119, 125, 135*n2*, 143*n4*
Hamitic hypothesis, 60
Harris, Olivia, 83
Hart, Gillian, 83
Head Tax (1917), 68
Henn, Jeanne Koopman, 98
Hutu, 61; codification of "tradition" by the Second Republic, 2; electoral victories, 72; elites, 2, 3; farming and, 65; in genocide, 109–126; identity development, 73; labor service and, 68; as "natural inhabitants," 60; as "natural rulers," 72; Northern, 2; peasant class of, 3; in postcolonial period, 72–78; power in hands of, 2; in precolonial period, 60–66; Southern, 2; submission to authority by, 70
Huye, 7, 10, 12, 13*fig*; beer sales in, 92; cooperative in, 54; owners in, 36, 37–40; piecework in, 37; sale of crops in, 90, 91*tab*

India: brick industry in, 29
Inheritance, 65–66; control of, 80; insecurity of, 85; land, 79–81, 141*n3*; siblings as adversaries, 80; unequal, 80, 81
Institutions: hierarchical, 2
Interahamwe, 114, 119, 120
International Monetary Fund, 110
Investment: in kilns, 22; in new technology, 44; reluctant, 45; risks and, 44; strategies, 45; of surplus, 82

Jackson, Cecile, 83
Jones, Bruce, 4

Kagame, Abbé Alexis, 60, 70
Kamanga, Calixte, 25
Kanama, 12
Karemeera Rwaka, 127*tab*
Kayibanda, Gregoire, 72, 73, 135*n2*
Keddie, James, 24, 29
Kibungo: employment in, 21
Kibuye: genocide in, 114
Kigali, 4; brick and roof tile industry in, 41; employment in, 21; genocide in, 114; owners in, 41
Kilns: adobe, 21, 24–25, 29, 30; brick, 21, *23;* capacity of, 22, 24, 30; Chinese, 25; clamp, 21, 22, *23,* 24, 29, 31, 137*n10;* cooling times, 24; drawing, 25; firing, 24, 25, 32*tab*, 36; fuel consumption, 22, 24, 29, 33*tab;* "improved," 24–25; industrial continuous, 25; intermittent, 22, *23,* 24; investment in, 22; joint, 30; knowledge needed to fire, 24, 25; loading, *23,* 24; permanent, 7, 10, 16, 24–25, 29; product breakage in, 31; profit on, 30; semicontinuous, 24–25, 29; stoking, 138*n2;* technology, 22; temporary, 12; tile, 21; underfiring and, 22
Kings: chronology of, 127*tab*
Kinship, 65–66; access to labor and, 85–86; authority in, 83; clans, 65; domestic relations and, 85–86; families, 83–85; gender relations in, 83; marriages, 83–85; patrilineal, 65; relations, 83
Kinyarwanda, 3

Labor: access to, 2, 3, 16, 85–86; agricultural, 44, 82, 92, 93; centralization of, 59, 77; children's, 86; in colonial period, 67; commodified nature of, 85; competition for, 36; conditions of, 36; contract, 70; control of, 82, 86; corvée, 68, 70, 73; costs, 30; day, 46; demands on, 67; division of, 36; exchange, 92; family, 3, 18, 56, 81–83; festive, 92; government provision of, 70–71; hired, 18, 35, 40, 56, 85, 92, 93; household, 18, 82; incentives for, 36; individual, 93; industrial, 93; lack of, 39–40; maintaining, 39–40; mobility, 39, 85; mobilization of, 68; obligatory, 68, 70, 74; organization, 2, 16, 19, 22, 35–57, 94–95; owner, 35; relations, 16, 18, 35, 71–72; reproduction of, 19, 86–88, 140*n2;* risks assumed by, 31, 44; seasonal, 46; self-exploitation and, 45; selling, 76, 77, 84, 92; service, 64, 67, 68, 73, 74; skilled, 36; strategies, 35–57; unpaid, 74; unskilled, 26, 36; wage, 18, 44, 70, 93, 138*n4;* women's, 3, 18, 82, 86–88, 88–89
Land: access to, 2, 3, 10, 16, 18, 30, 35, 36, 51, 53, 54, 56, 57, 65, 73, 74, 75, 81; appropriation of, 64; centralization of, 18, 59, 61, 77; chiefs, 63; clay, 18, 30, 35, 36, 51, 53; clearing, 26; clientage, 35, 64, 71, 115; common, 11*fig*, 13*fig*, 15*fig*, 17*fig*, 25, 59, 63, 65, 66, 71–72, 75, 92, 114; concentration, 4, 111; control of, 63, 85; distribution, 63, 65, 141*n3;* fragmentation of family holdings, 79–81; holdings, 4; inheritance and, 65, 79–81, 141*n3;* lineage, 61, 65, 74; monopolies on, 55; pasture, 63; patronage and, 36; pressure, 80, 81; private, 26, 56; public, 7; redistribution, 75; reform, 67; regional differences in use of, 36; rented, 40, 92; rights, 63, 65; tenure, 2, 18, 19, 30, 36, 45, 54, 59, 64, 65–66, 71–72, 74, 84
Landlessness, 4
Language, 3
Lem, Winnie, 86
Lemarchand, René, 61, 66, 68, 69, 71, 75, 112, 119, 134, 140*n5*
Lineage system, 65–66; agricultural, 65; appropriation of, 64; cattle-holding, 65; clientalism and, 63; clients of, 61;

destruction of, 64; effect on family inheritances, 84; erosion of, 63; function of, 75; lands, 61, 65, 74; marrying into, 61; power of, 64; termination of, 84; transformation of, 18
Lorber, Judith, 135*n1*
Lugan, Bernard, 84

MacGaffey, Janet, 99, 107
Mair, L., 60
Mamdani, Mahmood, 122
Manson, Jack, 29
Maquet, Jacques J., 60, 65, 70
Markets: access to, 18, 56; affluent, 7; nonmonetary, 84; peasant, 7, 18, 30, 50; poor, 18; rural, 6, 7, 30; small, 7; urban, 7, 18, 30, 36; wage labor, 70
Meschy, Lidia, 61, 66, 75, 76, 80
Mexico, 29
Mudandagizi, Vincent, 61, 63, 64, 65
Mujawamariya, Monique, 113
Mukandori, Josephine, 118, 119
Mukobanya (king), 62, 127*tab*
Musinga (king), 66, 69, 127*tab*

Nahimana, Ferdinand, 60, 61, 66
Ndadaye, Melchior, 112, 115, 117, 144*n10*
Ndahindurwa, 72
Ndahiro Cyamatare, 127*tab*
Ndahiro Ruyange, 62, 127*tab*
Ndoba, 127*tab*
Newbury, Catherine, 61, 65, 68, 69, 70, 71, 72, 77, 84, 110, 111, 113, 115, 123, 143*n2*
Newbury, David, 4, 61, 63, 84, 110, 113, 128, 143*n2*
Ngoma, 7, 10, 11*fig*, 12; clay digging in, 26; cooperative in, 51, 54; production strategies in, 45–51; sale of crops in, 90, 91*tab*
Nkundabashaka, Augustin, 86
Nongovernmental organizations, 10
Nyagahene, Antoine, 84
Nyiginya dynasty, 61
Nyiramashuko, Pauline, 108

Obbo, Christine, 99
Olson, Jennifer, 110
Out-migration, 70

Parmehutu Party, 72
Parpart, Jane, 98
Patrilineal clans, 3, 65
Peres Blancs, 67
Pfunda, 12, 15*fig*, 16; brick and roof tile industry in, 40–42, 41; clay digging in, 26; cooperative in, 53; owners in, 36, 41; sale of crops in, 90, 91*tab*
Piecework, 12, 16, 18, 22, 31, 36, 40, 87, 93; advantages of, 44; capitalist enterprises and, 43–45; drawbacks of, 45; enthusiasm for, 43; quality and, 45; as working for self, 43, 48
Political: clientage, 73–74; exclusion, 124; ideology, 74; manipulation, 118–121; opposition, 3, 111; reform, 68; relations, 2; repression, 110; structures, 73–74
Polygyny, 83, 84, 85, 99, 142*n5*
Population: density, 4, 64; growth, 110; rural, 4
Postcolonial period, 72–73; ethnic violence in, 72, 77; transformations during, 2; turbulence during, 72
Pottier, Johan, 86, 89, 117, 139*n13*
Poverty, 89
Power: access to, 2, 3, 16, 125; centralization of, 2, 3, 18, 59, 61, 64, 71, 77; ethnicity and, 2; lineages, 63, 64; monopolies of, 68; paternal, 81; regional exclusion and, 2; relations, 2
Precolonial period, 60–66; Butare, 10, 12, 21; changing nature of, 61; exploitation during, 60; frontiers of kingdom in, 61; Hutu peoples in, 60–66; lineages in, 61; social relations in, 18; transformations during, 2; tribute in, 62, 63, 64; Tutsi peoples in, 60–66
Prioul, Christian, 4
Production: access to labor and, 81–83; agricultural, 18; capitalist, 16, 18, 35,

Production *(continued)*
  36–42, 134*n1*; capital needs in, 31; cooperatives and, 16, 51–55; customers for, 42; economy of scale in, 30–31; family control of, 84; firing and drawing kiln, 25, 27, 29, 36; forming, 27; for government construction, 21–22; hacking in, 27; for housing, 21–22; labor process for, 25–29, 31; land inheritance and, 81–83; large-scale, 31; marriage and, 82; means of, 3, 18, 35, 53, 98; molding product, 25, 26–27; owner involvement in, 18, 36–40; peasant, 18, 19, 36, 45–51, 56, 83–85; preparation for firing, 25, 27, 32*tab*; shaping/trimming, 27, *28*; skills needed, 30; small peasant, 16; small-scale, 45–51, 83–85; strategies, 45–51; tools for, 26; transportation to kiln, 27, 29; variations in, 30; winning clay, 25–26, 32*tab*, 36
Prunier, Gérard, 143*n1*

Racism, 2
Radio-Télévision Libre Milles Collines, 113
Reader, J., 62
Religion, 3
Rennie, J.K., 61, 128
Reporters Sans Frontières, 61
Republics, 2, 3, 73–76, 77, 123; political structure, 73–74; social structure, 73–74
Reseau Zéro, 120
Resources: access to, 18, 73, 74, 81, 125; centralization of, 18; control of, 97–108, 98, 107; paternal control of, 18
Reyntjens, Filip, 72, 73, 111, 112, 113, 114, 115
Rights: customary, 75; to dig clay, 57; human, 119, 120, 125; land, 63, 65; lineage, 75; property, 65; of women, 65
Roberts, Penelope, 107

Robertson, Claire, 98, 99, 135*n1*
Ruanda-Urundi, 66, 129
Rudahigwa (king), 69, 70, 127*tab*
Ruhashya, 7
Ruhengeri, 12, 16; cooperative in, 55; genocide in, 114
Rujugira (king), 127*tab*, 140*n3*
Rutarindwa (king), 66, 127*tab*
Rwabukumba, Joseph, 61, 63, 64, 65
Rwanda: Arusha Accords and, 112; assimilation in, 61; authoritarian systems in, 69; as Belgian Protectorate, 3, 66, 67–68, 129, 131–132; as "caste system," 3; Catholic Church in, 67; claim of no ethnic differences in, 122; class and gender in, 87, 106–108; clientalism in, 60; Coalition pour le Défense de la République in, 112; colonial period in, 66–76; conquest in, 61; corporate perception of ethnicity in, 123; corruption in, 72, 73, 110, 113; coups d'etat in, 72; current regime in, 121–126; democratization in, 1, 111; demographics, 4, 6; development aid to, 4; as "Developmental State," 74; division into military districts, 67; drought in, 110; economic crisis in, 90, 110, 143*n2*; economic growth in, 1, 138*n7*; economic restructuring in, 73, 110; elections in, 72; ethnic propaganda in, 111–112, 113; export revenues, 4; foreign debt in, 4; genocide in, 109–126; geographic contexts of, 3–4; as German colony, 3, 66–67; Hamitic hypothesis in, 60; as hierarchical state, 60; households in, 83–85; Hutu Power extremism in, 61; indirect rule in, 68; Interahamwe in, 114, 119, 120; international community and, 111, 119, 120, 121; kinship relations in, 83–85; lack of resources in, 111; lineages in, 61; manufacturing in, 6; media in, 112, 113, 124–125; "metaconflict" in, 61;

Nyiginya dynasty in, 61; opposition in, 3; Parmehutu Party in, 72; patrilineal clans in, 3; political contexts, 5*map;* political opposition in, 111; political repression in, 110; postcolonial period in, 72–73; precolonial military organization, 63; precolonial period, 2; precolonial period in, 2; racist ideology in, 72; rationalization of dictatorship in, 112; rebuilding, 121; reproduction of patterns of past regimes in, 121–126; Rwandan Patriotic Front in, 3, 73, 110, 113, 114, 121, 122, 124, 125, 143*n1*, 143*n4;* Social Revolution in, 2, 135*n2;* state projects in, 68; status of women in, 98–99; structural adjustment in, 2, 110, 111; succession in, 3; system of *prestations* in, 70; "time of the whip" in, 68–71; Two Republics in, 2, 3, 73–76, 77, 123; unemployment in, 110, 111
Rwandan Patriotic Front, 2, 3, 73, 110, 112, 113, 114, 121, 122, 124, 125, 143*n1*, 143*n4*
Rwanga, Charles, 25

Samembe (king), 127*tab*
Sector, formal, 6
Sector, informal, 6
Sector, service, 6
Self-provisioning, 89–94; brick and roof tile industry and, 90–94
Sibomana, André, 112, 124, 144*n12*
Social: relations, 2, 18; structures, 73–74
Social Revolution, 2
Stanley, Henry Morton, 129
Staudt, Kathleen, 98
Stichter, Sharon, 98
Strategies: hiring help, 45, 47–48; hiring labor/work with laborers, 45, 50–51; investment, 45; labor, 35–57; production, 45–51; sharing labor process, 45–46; variety of, 16; working alone/with group, 45, 48–49
Structural adjustment, 2, 110

Tanzania, 4, 141*n10*
Techniques, 21–31; introduction of, 21–22
Tiles: floor, 24, 42; formation, 27; forming, 36; laying out, 27; life span of, 30; market for, 30; molds, 27; need for greater care in preparation, 26; shaping, 27; as sideline, 42; skills needed, 24; trimming, 27, *28;* unfired, 49
Tools, 26; common, 56; digging, 29; simple, 31, 56
Transportation: by children, 38; of product to kiln, 27, 29; by unskilled labor, 36
Tutsi, 61; aristocratic clans of, 2; assimilation of, 65; colonialism and, 64; division of, 69; elites, 65; favoritism for, 62, 69; Hamitic hypothesis and, 60; in genocide, 109–126; herding and, 65; modern faction, 69; as outsider group, 60; peasant class of, 3; in postcolonial period, 72–78; in precolonial period, 60–64; redistribution of resources of, 74; in Rwandan Patriotic Front, 73; traditional faction, 69; violence against, 69
Twa, 3

Uganda, 1, 4, 79–81, 107, 138*n7*, 142*n2*
United Nations: Educational, Scientific and Cultural Organization, 4; Industrial Development Organization, 22, 24, 29; intervention in postcolonial era, 72; peacekeeping mission, 120; pressure on Belgium, 71; Security Council, 120
Uvin, Peter, 4, 111, 119
Uwilingiyimama, Agathe, 120

Vansina, Jan, 60, 61, 64, 115, 128
Vidal, Claudine, 61, 64, 69, 84, 85, 141*n6*
Voss, Joachim, 84, 87

Wagner, Michele, 122
Watts, Michael, 83–85

Whitehead, Anne, 83, 87
Women: access to cash, 87; agricultural labor by, 3, 82; cash-earning projects, 141*n11;* circumscribed rights of, 98–99; control of income by, 87; control of labor, 88–89; control of land, 140*n9,* 141*n3;* control of resources by, 97–108; enterprise owners, 19; *femmes libre,* 99; inferiority of, 65; labor and, 18; legal status of, 98–99; married, 98–99, 140*n9,* 141*n3;* ownership of production by, 97–108; ownership of resources, 18; property rights of, 65; responsibilities of, 18, 79, 82, 86–88; social expectations of, 98–99; stereotypes of, 97–108; unmarried, 99, 100–103; violence against, 88–89; vulnerability of family position, 99; widowed, 99, 141*n3,* 142*n2*

World War I, 66
World War II, 71

Yanagisako, Sylvia, 83
Yuhi Gahindiro, 63, 127*tab*

Zaire. *See* Democratic Republic of Congo

Printed in the United States
106214LV00003B/177/A